ACROSS THE EVERGLADES

A Play for the Screen

By BUDD SCHULBERG

What Makes Sammy Run?
The Harder They Fall
The Disenchanted
Some Faces in the Crowd
Waterfront
A Face in the Crowd
A Play for the Screen Developed from the
Novelette "Your Arkansas Traveler"

Across the Everglades

Across
the
Everglades

A play for the screen
by

Budd Schulberg

RANDOM HOUSE, NEW YORK

Frontispiece: Stuart Schulberg, *left*, and Budd Schulberg, *right*
Photograph by courtesy of Muky

Library of Congress Catalog Card Number: 58–12429

Manufactured in the United States of America

Schulberg, Budd. Across the Everglades;
a play for the screen. 1958. 126p. illus.
Random, $2.95.

In a lengthy introduction the author tells of
his fascination with the Everglades and in
the play itself he pictures the region as it
was in the early twentieth century. Walt
Murdock, protector of rookeries and hero of
the play, finds Cottonmouth, head of the
illegal bird killers, a wily opponent but in
the finale Walt is victorious. The characters
are not memorable but the mysterious beauty
of the setting is graphically portrayed.

812.5 792 Across the Everglades (Motion picture)   58-12429

CERF

INTRODUCTION

BY

BUDD SCHULBERG

"But where do you get your ideas?" asked a sympathetic stranger as he crowded me into a corner at the cocktail party. This is an occupational hazard that every writer knows.

The conscientious answer tends to be circuitous, not at all a simple cause-and-effect but a whole complex of experiences distilled into memories. Every writer knows there is no such thing as a sudden burst of inspiration. A story is something that happens to you, related to something else that happened to you and keeps on happening to you, that even manages to happen in spite of you. It may be an even more mysterious and complicated process than having a baby, and frequently the period of gestation is much longer than a mere nine months. Nine years is more like it.

Nine years ago, vacationing in Key West, my wife and I decided to take a vacation from our vacation. It was to be a fishing trip, out to Cay Sal, in the straits of Florida, between Key West and the coast of Cuba. An old man of the sea by the name of Hemingway had told us of the heavyweight sport fish that waited to be taken in the deep waters around that towering rock.

But storm warnings were up, day after day, while our charter boat, *The Tramp,* and her leathery, daredevil skipper, Bob Ikerd, waited patiently for us at their slip on the Gulf side of Lower Matecumbe, a link in the green chain of Florida Keys.

Once we even ventured out on the Atlantic side of the Keys, but heavy seas drove us back to shore. By this time my wife and I and our two boys, and some friends, were established aboard *The Tramp*. Stirred by sea fever and tropical wanderlust, we implored the skipper to take us *somewhere*.

"We could run inside, across Florida Bay, over to Cape Sable, and up the rivers running into the Glades," Ikerd said.

A little while later we were threading our way through the mangrove keys that dot the shallow water of the Bay, off the southern coast of Florida. A sign rising out of the yellow-green water informed us that we were entering the Everglades National Wild Life Refuge. We sailed past rookeries, small mangrove islands safe from marauding coons and snakes and the other relentless enemies of the birds. Here we saw our first plume birds—the long-necked, immaculately white American egret; the smaller, aristocratic snowy egret; the great blue herons; squadrons of white pelicans; and even a few roseate spoonbills, birds ungainly and broad-billed on the ground but beautiful in flight, their wings so delicately pinked, their underwings as crimson as a tropical Florida sunset. Almost extinct forty years ago, when the plume hunters were slaughtering plume birds of every color for the flourishing ladies' millinery fad, they were now protected by the National Audubon Society. The spoonbills—or pink curlews—we saw were part of a community of some two hundred that was slowly restoring a rare and beautiful breed in this seldom frequented water wilderness.

Hour by hour the fascination of this unique and practically unknown corner of America caught our imagination. We began to forget about the marlin and the dolphin and the piscatory triumphs that might have awaited us on the deeper, ocean side of the Keys. Instead of being gamefish hunters, we were being converted into bird watchers and neophyte Evergladians.

INTRODUCTION

The lure of the place, the quality of its silence, its sun-drenched loneliness, its unpopulated shoreline, its strange, still largely unexplored interior, drew us on. We passed the south-ernmost fishing village on the mainland of the United States, Flamingo, and heard racy stories of its unruly neighbor, Snake Bight, said to be infested with outlaws, moonshiners, smugglers, squatters, seagoing frontiersmen as lawless, as untamed as Billy the Kid and his trigger-ready pony boys. "Snake Bight is a frontier beyond the frontier," somebody said. Later I was to hear the New York waterfront described exactly in those words. But the metropolitan harbor represented organized plunder and corruption. Snake Bight, a ragtail community of crudely constructed shacks, on buttonwood stilts, built out over the shallows of south Florida's land's-end, reflected an altogether different kind of lawlessness. Not well-organized labor racketeering but a primitive, anti-social, anarchy reigned here. From the days of pirates to rum-runners, the Everglades had been a natural hideout—a hostile, insect-and-reptile-infested jungle of mangrove rivers and trackless saw grass.

We rounded the southwestern point of Cape Sable and followed the beach that ran on and on to the north, nearly twenty miles of dazzling white sand under a boundless blue sky decorated with great cream-puff clouds. Here, cut off from the mainland—if the brackish and fresh-water swampland of the Glades can ever be described so solidly—was one of the great uninhabited beaches of the world, its scorching yellow-white horizontal broken only by the occasional palms that would qualify it for membership in any self-respecting group of deserted South Sea islands. A mere eighty miles as the crow—or the white ibis—flies from the Babylonian luxury hotels of Miami Beach, here there was not a single cottage or fishing shack, mile after mile. Yet the beach looked so inviting that we were prompted to ask the question, What would stop anyone from building a seashore retreat here and coming over by boat or flying in by seaplane? Our skipper grinned and gave us this intriguing answer:

"A couple of years ago a dentist from Miami came over here and built himself a beach house. The weekend after he finished it he came back to enjoy it and found every stick of furniture gone. With some friends he hiked back into the Whitewater Bay country but couldn't find a living soul. Glade squatters, moving in like locusts, had simply vanished. In those Glades it's easy to do, if you know your way. The dentist didn't give up. He built all the furniture in. He brought stronger locks. But when he returned, the locks had been broken and all the built-in furniture was stripped away. Even his jeep beach buggy was stripped of its tires, its gas and some vital parts. And yet there didn't seem to be a sign of human life for miles. I took him over here on this boat on his last trip. I put him and his family ashore, and since I had run all night, I came back to *The Tramp* to get some sleep. From down in my cabin I heard a small boat approaching. I got up and sneaked a look through the port hole. A small boatload of filthy-looking, bearded squatters was coming alongside. I waited until they boarded—evidently they were bent on doing the same thing to *The Tramp* as they had been doing to the doc's beach house. Then I came roaring up with a revolver in my hand and threatened to blow their heads off if they didn't get off my boat. They got. But I told the dentist, beautiful as the beach was, I wouldn't try to start a beach colony there. Those squatters were almost as dangerous as the Carib Indians who fought off the Spaniards when they tried to land here four hundred years ago. In a way you can't blame them. They lived there when nobody else wanted it. They put up with the redbugs and the mosquitoes and the snakes. They didn't have papers to prove it, they didn't homestead it, because they could live off the land—the fish and the deer and the birds, wild turkeys, curlew, heron. But they felt it belonged to them by natural rights. A lot of them were second and third generation. They were like the Seminole Indians. They had come to the ends of America to be left alone and live their own life. And here we were, barging in on them."

We sailed on, leaving the naked, provocative beach to be washed by the lazy surf of the Gulf as it had—and looking no different—for tens of thousands of years. Now the shoreline was fringed with mangrove—but giant black mangrove a hundred feet high. We came to the mouth of a great river—Shark River it was—one of the many unknown rivers, including Lostman's, Harney's, Broad, Roger's, Barron's, cutting inland from the Gulf and subtly changing from salt to brackish to sweet as they mingle with the flow of fresh water pouring out in a southwesterly direction from Lake Okeechobee, a weird healthy-water swamp hole a hundred and twenty-five miles in circumference, the natural reservoir that spills its overflow contents for a hundred Venetian miles south into the Bay and southwest into the Gulf.

Shark River is wide and silent. The mangrove grips its banks like the gnarled claws of the eagles that perch in its top branches. The river bank is composed of countless thousands of these gnarled claws or thickened fingers—thrusting down into the mud and holding on. They are called the land-builder, for these entwined trunks accumulate around them fallen leaves and floating jetsam and silt until a kind of primordial land is formed, providing organic hospitality for other life forms. These are ancient trees, and around them minute by minute, day by day, decade by decade, millennium by millennium new land is forming. The miracle is taking place—if you have the imagination to picture it—before your eyes, and you speculate that the world might have looked something like this in the first days of creation when the world was all water and the first land was beginning to rise out of the sea. The water is shallow here and our boat moves slowly. The only sound is the lapping against the hull, and the cries of the red-headed or pileated woodpeckers and other birds. The water is full of catfish, and a fishhawk dives for one, only to be driven off by an eagle, a noble bird to look upon but a scavenging great thief of a bird who uses his size and reach, like a street-corner bully, to grab his prey from lesser birds. The larger fish eat the smaller fish and the birds eat them both and the larger birds prey on the lesser birds and the alligators grab them all in their slow-fast, sleep-awake primordial way. Eagles and alligators, herons, deadly water moccasins and wild orchids, we see them all as we move up river into the narrower channels, where the water is a brackish brown, an ugly, beautiful color, and again you feel that down there in that amber ooze lies Caliban. Among the prehistoric garfish and the dog-faced catfish and the sub-merging 'gators, lurks not only Caliban but God, for surely He is not only in the heavens but down there in the muck out of which the first life spawned.

From the Shark River we have moved into the Little Shark, and now the waterways twist themselves into a desperate guessing-game labyrinth—each rivulet forking off in three, four, five directions, curling around identical mangrove tangles. No wonder the Seminole Indians, in their legendary struggle for survival against element-ravaged American regiments, could pole off into hidden waterways and disappear into the flat, oppressive, secretive land- and water-scape of the Glades.

The day passes in eventful uneventfulness. Our boys boat a mess of catfish with bread for bait—a far cry from the flashing Gulf stream trolling for sailfish in the blue water on the Atlantic side. A swallow-tailed kite—so aptly named—power dives over and over again to within a few feet of the nose of an eagle threatening her nest. An awakened ten-foot alligator splashes out of its crawl. A number of two-foot 'gators watch us with their cold slit-eyes raised a fraction of an inch above the water level.

Now *The Tramp,* a forty-four-footer, could move inland no further. So we lowered the skiff, with the bravado intention of following these waterways inland, northeast, in the general direction of Miami, as far as we could go. Soon we were leaving the Chinese puzzle of mangrove keys and brackish channels behind. The saline marshes were giving way to a more varied fresh-water jungle of dwarf cypress, palms, live oak, pine, and the indomitable yellow-green saw grass that marks the true Everglades. Search your dictionaries, and you will find no satisfactory definition or description of this generic American word. The clinical words of Webster inform you that a glade is a clearing, or open space, even a shiny place in the forest or the sky. But this is tall grass, strange grass, a sharp three-sided blade grass, one of the oldest forms of green vegetation known to man, a fierce grass that can slice your clothing and your flesh. Look across it and you might be looking at a midwestern wheat field, a million acres of yellow-green strands bending gently to the breeze. But then look down and you see water shining through the grass:—Pa-hay-okee—grassy water—the Indians called this region, and that is the best description of Everglades, grassy water or watery grass and, perhaps because it seems to run on and on forever, as in a surrealist landscaped dream, the first maps identified this country as "ever glades."

Marjory Stoneman Douglas, the Everglades' affectionate and gifted biographer, has called this "a river of grass," and in truth this liquid jungle is a river without banks, the slight down-tilting of flat lower Florida allowing the water to spread for seventy miles in breadth as it runs its hundred miles from the great lake to the sea. But this is not all water, for the boundless river of grass is punctuated with tens of thousands of hammocks

—or small islands rising out of the shallow water and grass— high ground providing relief from the fierce monotony of saw grass. These hammocks are fertile, and from them rise great stands of cypress, that ancient scarecrow tree that plays dead but manages to outlive every other tree on earth. And there are pines and tall palms and great oaks festooned with Spanish moss. It was to these hammocks that the Seminoles withdrew when the white men broke their treaties and pressed them back from the coasts and south from the solid land north of Okeechobee. On these hammocks they planted bananas and squash and mangoes. From these hidden islands in their un-charted saw-grass sea they fought a thirty years' war, moving their wives and children with them in their long, slender, shal-low-draft cypress dugouts, a war of hit-run-and-hide that con-founded American troops for generations, and finally ground to an uneasy halt—the only official war the United States en-gaged in and never won.

It was not only the unbending pride of Osceola and Billy Bowlegs and other Seminole chieftains that prevailed. The ter-rain also prevailed. As you move through the crazy-quilt pat-tern of hammocks, as you step ashore (as I have done) and find an abandoned still, or a brand-new one with the grain freshly poured, or a nest of baby ground-rattlers, or instead of a poison snake a poison tree like the manchineel that will burn your skin, blind you and in time destroy your mucous membrane, you feel you have discovered at last a wilderness that man has never conquered, that defies the best of our efforts to subdue it, civilize it, tame it. Black bears, panthers, wildcats stalk its prairies. The dainty, nimble dwarf deer abound. At night the frogs set up a million-throated croaking thunder. The alligators raise their hollow bark. A limpkin, a night heron, an owl stabs the darkness. And if you have the poor luck or poor judgment to come too near a hammock or a mangrove shore, the mosquitoes hum their buzzing welcome to the feast they are preparing for you, or rather on you. You learn to brush them off, cracker-style, rather than to swat them, flail at them, lose your temper at them as we do in the north. Like the saw grass and the cypress and the alligator and the garfish and the water and the unbroken skyscape, they were here before man and are a part of the timelessness—nature's insistence and epic right to put man in his place—that makes an exploration of the Glades a spiritual experience as well as a physical adventure.

On our return from the saw-grass prairie and the narrow creeks low-bridged with vine-covered branches, we suffered one of those crises better suited to the hairy-chested men's magazines than to this consideration of how dramatic forms and themes gestate and develop in the mind of a writer. The star game fish of the Glades rivers and lakes is the muscular, stubborn tarpon, and we slowed our skiff in Tarpon Bay to try our luck with plugs and trolling lines. The scene we found was like a chapter from Lowell Thomas. There were tarpon all right, hundreds of them, hundred-pound six-footers rolling, breaking, diving in a boiling circle. We trolled through them expecting to be jerked out of the boat, but nothing happened. We cast a plug into the boiling middle of that great circle, but nothing happened. They would literally slap against the side of the boat. We could see them flashing their silvery power a few feet from us, just below the surface, but they rolled away from our hooks. The process was fascinating in its frustration, and when we finally decided that they were either spawning, playing or gorged on the plentiful shrimp, the sun was going down.

We cruised for half an hour, with evening closing around us as the sun slipped down behind the clustered mangrove keys. A familiar mangrove formation appeared again. We were sure of it, for we had remarked on it sometime earlier. We were going around in circles. Our skipper knew his way through the

Florida Keys and the Caribbean but he had never been up here before. His chart was of no help, for this interior had not even been charted yet. He admitted that he was lost. My wife looked at me. Our children were on the larger boat. Another half hour. Gas was running low. Someone remembered that a famous jockey from Hialeah—Snider—had been lost in this section and never found again. The Glades are rife with legends of murders—bodies disposed of and never seen again—death by exposure, redbugs, red ants, mosquitoes. We stared into the dark, matted, crooked-fingered world of the mangroves. The black-green mangrove and the dark brown water and the brooding evening sky was all, the dawn and the dying twilight of the world, the once-was, the here and the hereafter. Even in my fear, and I still remember how frightened I became, I felt a terrible fascination in it. These Everglades had drawn us deep into their inexorable, primeval dream.

At last, half an hour later, we noticed a landmark, a single tree on a toy island about twenty-five feet in circumference that gave us the general direction of our boat. We shouted through the darkness. The welcome voices of our children and the mate came faintly back. A few minutes later we were back on board, toasting our relief and good fortune in rum. After that, we learned—like seasoned Gladesmen—to leave white rags on the mangrove branches to mark our wanderings.

Another year, another abortive fishing trip along the keys led to a curious morning that moved me to further wonder about the Glades. A sudden, slashing rain and a hard blow out of the northwest canceled out the day's fishing and drove us into a ramshackle bar that was little more than sheets of corrugated tin fastened rather precariously together. Inside, half a dozen unshaven, dirty-looking fishermen were immobilized not only by the storm but by the quantities of whiskey that they obviously had been drinking since the dawn nor'wester, or quite possibly for longer than that. They were actually harmonizing in hoarse, flat, carefree voices, "Old Black Joe." They eyed us with bleak suspicion as we invaded their bar in our clean, bright-colored sports wear. One character in particular loomed above the rest. He looked—and turned out to be—part Indian, tall, wiry, bearded, with beady and baleful black eyes and a trickle of dry blood running in an unappealing half-moon from the corner of his mouth to his chin.

We were just remarking to each other that the Indian looked like one of those exaggerated heavies in the Chaplin movies, when, perhaps, suspecting that we were amusing ourselves at his expense, the Indian singled me out and raised his voice: "Hey, you, are you a Jew?" The bartender, nervously back of his hand, cautioned me not to answer him. "He's a knife fighter, a troublemaker, he's always trying to cut somebody up in here." But the big fellow was answering his startling rhetorical question: "If you're a Jew, I'm an A-rab."

It was the year of the Arab invasion of Israel. But I never expected a tiny skirmish of that distant war to be fought here in this remote corner of the Florida Keys on the edge of the Everglades. The half-breed fisherman (I realize I'm falling into *Western* clichés here, but this is the way it happened) challenged me again, and calling vaguely on some old prep-school training about attack being the best defense, I went over to him and said, in a small voice I did my best to keep steady, that I objected to the way he was talking to me. He eyed me up and down and drew his fishing knife, an ugly six-inch blade. "Where do you come from, New York?" It is difficult to recapture the contempt, the hatred he put into that word. I said, no, I was raised in California, and was now living on a farm in Pennsylvania. "I never been to Miami," he announced proudly, "and I never been to Key West." I said that that was fine, nobody was insisting that he go to Miami or Key West. He thought about that a moment. "To hell with New York and Miami," he said. "I belong right here." I said I didn't care too much for New York or Miami either. That's why my wife and I had been vacationing here at Matecumbe. He thought that over for a moment. "Do yuh drink?" What else would I be doing in a bar at ten o'clock in the morning, I said. "I'll buy you a drink," he said. We each tossed off a shot, wham, real *Western* style, and then I said I'd buy him a drink, and then he said he'd buy me a drink, and he kept watching me as I tossed mine down as fast as he tossed his.

It was a contest, and I could see out of the corner of my eye his group and my group watching anxiously from farther down the bar. We kept it up until we had each spent a five-dollar bill. Then, still holding the knife on me, he said, "Let's sit down." We sat opposite each other at a small table across the aisle from the bar, continuing to drink and explore each other. "You wanna go fishin', I'll take you out right now," he said. I reminded him that a gale was still blowing outside and storm warnings were up. "Don't matter, I c'n handle my boat in any kind of weather." I said I'd rather wait for the storm to blow itself out. "If you come out with me you gotta remember one thing," he said, "I'm the captain. If you don't do what I say, I c'n put you in chains." I said I preferred to wait for the boat I had already chartered. "Okay, suit ye'self," he said. "I don't need you. I don't need anybody." He reached into his pocket and pulled out a thick wad of bills. "I got five hundred dollars here. Every cent of it I made myself. It's mine and no son of a bitch is going to take it away from me." He gestured at me with the knife. By this time my answers had become somewhat automatic. Where he was wrong was in thinking anybody wanted to take his five hundred away from him, I said. Was there anybody in this bar who gave a damn about his five hundred? He had earned it and he was welcome to it. I told him to put it back in his pocket before he lost it through drink and carelessness.

Suddenly he leaned over and tapped me fondly on the knee. "Yah know, I like you, stranger. You're my friend, Le's have another drink." We were on our fifteenth straight whiskey. The knife wagged uncertainly in the general direction of my belly. If we had become such friends, I suggested, did he have to keep that knife poking at me? He looked around, squint-eyed and frowning at his cronies at the bar. Then he leaned across the table until his bloodied, slobbering mouth was at my ear. "I'll tell you why I gotta hang on to this knife," he stage-whispered. "I come over from on the East Coast, see. When I'm over here on the West Coast, I gotta be *armed*." It took me a few moments to realize that by West Coast he didn't mean California, or even the west coast of Florida. He meant the west coast of Matecumbe, an island half a mile wide. I told him I thought he was quite safe here in the bar—by some alcoholic alchemy I now seemed to be bolstering him against his fears—but he refused to sheath his blade. Instead, he leaned over the table again until the point of the knife was touching my smoothly designed sports shirt. "Look, we're friends?" Yes, I said, we're friends. "We're friends now?" I said, yes, we were friends now. "Okay, friends." Yes, I said, yes, yes, friends. He put his large, mud-grimed hand out. We shook hands, overly formal, like Secretaries of rival commonwealths. "Now le's go out on the dock 'n fight, jes' for fun," he offered. "Jes' a couple friends fightin' f'fun. I'll get you a knife so it'll be fair." He grinned at me and I noticed how small his eyes were in his large, unfriendly face. He was pressing his invitation to this congenial battle of fishing knives on the wind-swept dock when one of the fishermen came over.

"Okay, Wes, you've been bothering this fellow long enough. Now go on back to the bar where you belong."

To my surprise, my knife-happy friend rose and went obediently back to his corner of the bar. I introduced myself to the rugged-looking, broad-shouldered, whiskied fisherman who had come to my rescue. To my amazement, he said, "My name is Bud Kirk. I've read your books. I come from Collier City over on Marco Island." This is one of the Ten Thousand Islands in the Gulf, marking the western approach to the Everglades. Bud and I returned to the bar and talked for an hour. If I was interested in realism, gutty subjects, Americana, as he felt I was from reading some of my novels, he said, I should come to Collier City, a lawless community where every man was his own law, and where a Federal man never even dared to enter. Desperate men on the lam were welcome in Collier City, Bud Kirk told me; it was a kind of village of the lost, physically and socially cut off from the mainland of Florida. It had been a favorite refuge for rum-runners and smugglers. Killings went unpunished. Outsiders had little chance of survival. It was not so much depraved as amoral. "There is nothing in Faulkner or Caldwell that could touch it for flaunting of the accepted ways of society. There are shacks where three generations live together, with grandfathers who never sober up and think nothing of going to bed with their granddaughters." It was a place, he said, where the id took precedence over the ego.

I stared in disbelief at this scaly, unkempt fisherman who looked as disreputable as the half-breed knife fighter and yet whose language was seasoned with references and ideas that would have seemed more suitable on a college campus than in this rough hangout on the Keys. Where had he come from? Surely he was not really one of the local fishermen. He came from Buffalo, he admitted, some twenty years earlier. He had come down to Marco with a wealthy man who needed a winter in the American tropics for his health. He had stayed on, living in a tent, picking up a few dollars as a bouncer in a

Marco bar, one of the toughest in America, where Saturday night "cuttin's" were a weekly social event. He had been a commercial fisherman, an Audubon warden, an alligator hunter. Eventually he married the niece of the woman who ran Marco Island like a benevolently dictatorial queen. He had roamed all over the Glades by skiff and on foot, hunting deer, 'gator, bear and plume birds for food. Why was he here, in camouflage so to speak, blending in with these unreconstructed local fishermen and hunters? "I can sum it up in one word," I remember his saying. "Protest." He would say no more. How deep his words sank in I only realized ten years later when they found their way into one of the climactic scenes of my film play, *Across the Everglades*.

Through the years I kept track of Bud Kirk, for I believed him to be that morning—and ten years later, still do—one of the most interesting and versatile and enriching people I ever met. He is—if he would only write his experiences—a kind of Everglades' Thoreau—a self-taught archeologist, Glades' historian, marine biologist, naturalist, humanist. With his family he lives on an Indian oyster-shell mound at the little harbor of Goodland on the southeast side of Marco. He has carried out excavations in this shell mound, scientifically noting the strata so that he can date the pottery and weapons of the ancient Carib Indians who were here in pre-Colombian times. He has sent his finds to the various museums of Florida. As an Audubon warden he risked his life to protect the plume birds against local hunters, who recognized no authority except that of their own shotguns. But he was not exactly an Audubon model, for he was hard-drinking, hard-living in those days. He himself killed alligators illegally to supplement his income, and he maintained an affectionate tolerance for the Gladesmen who lived the life they were born to and saw nothing wrong in killing off the birds who were part of *their* Everglades.

Eventually I thought of Bud Kirk as a gold mine not just of material in the crude sense but of complexity of the sort that could make my story of the Everglades not merely cops-and-robbers, warden versus plume hunter, a *Western* moved to the Badlands of the Far South, but a human drama in which right and wrong blend into and overlap each other. The Everglades is rich in this complexity. Bud had been a bouncer, a bar-fighter, a drunk, a seemingly calloused member of the demoralized mullet and mackerel fishing fraternity who roam the Florida west coast. But he also had taken a year off from fishing to study marine biology at the University of Miami. He had been offered a job as a qualified member of an archeological expedition heading for India. He could walk you through the knee-deep muck of an overgrown mangrove swamp, infested with mosquitoes and offering murky hospitality to the dreaded cottonmouths, and transform it into a glen of unbelievable wonder and beauty. He knew the Latin names of all the wild orchids and could spot a bloom in what seemed to be nothing but dense overgrowth a hundred feet away. He knew the name and habits of everything that grew in this swamp. And under the spell of his enthusiasm, what had seemed a dank and forbidding swamp in which you feared to walk became something as natural and beguiling as Walden Pond. Bud Kirk goes out into that swamp and walks alone for hours, "just to rest my nerves, something like walking through a cathedral," and as he tells you this and you look around at the hushed shadows of the place, its solitary strangeness begins to grow on you and you learn still another lesson in the unfolding, never-ending study of the Glades.

Over the ten years between my first trip into Shark River and the moment of writing this introduction, I've gone into the Glades a dozen times, for fishing, vacation, sightseeing, and research for travel articles. I've talked to people on all sides of the Glades' question, for the disposal of the Everglades is still a live issue, centering around a new bill to be introduced in Congress. Dan Beard, superintendent of the new Everglades National Park—a million and a quarter acres from Homestead to Cape Sable and from Lostman's River to Flamingo on Florida Bay—is proud of the fact that this wilderness is to be protected and preserved from the inroads of land speculators who would drain it and sell it off for farm land and subdivisions, thereby driving out of Florida and the American continent some of the rarest wildlife in the world. The Park is a fabulous zoo without bars, where roads are now being built and boardwalks out over swamps where tropical birds and reptiles can be seen at close range. Dan Beard hopes the Park boundaries can be extended north another twenty miles from Lostman's River to Barron River on which stands Everglades City, less a city than a quaint, time-forgotten fishing village of dirt streets and one-story western-type buildings that bear a striking resemblance to the Florida of fifty years ago.

Listen to Dan Beard and you are convinced that he and his Department of Interior colleagues are striking a noble blow for conservation in maintaining this unique American wilderness and making it accessible at last to great numbers of American tourists.

But listen to the descendants of the original settlers and you begin to appreciate the sad fact that there has never been an easy, decisive line between progress and status quo, or between a society of law and order and a society of lawless self-sufficiency. Snake Bight is gone now, and so is Collier City, and Dan Beard will tell you that "we have the squatter problem practically licked." But the grandson of a squatter, guiding you on a fishing trip through the Ten Thousand Islands, tells you a bitter story of his grandfather, who raised his family near the mouth of Lostman's River, a solitary man whose deed to his house and land was his own hands and his own resources to withstand the elements. "When the Park was set up he refused to move, so finally one day when he was off fishin', those damn wardens just moved in an' burned 'im out," your guide says in his nasal cracker singsong that is unlike any dialect I ever heard. And the mate tells another story—how a friend of his, descended from one of the plume-hunting tribes that were wiping out the birds half a century ago, was hunting 'gators inside the Park boundaries when he was apprehended by a young Park warden. The warden knew that Billy B.—as we'll call him—had as many as thirty 'gators skinned out nearby, a nice haul at the going black-market rate of five dollars a foot. "I'm going to have to follow you and confiscate those hides," the neophyte warden said. "Go ahead, follow me," Billy B. invited. "I'll be the last man you ever follow." The warden hesitated and then went back to report his problem to Dan Beard's headquarters in Homestead.

"Billy wasn't talkin' fer show," my fishing guide chuckled. "He would o' killed him fer damn sure. One thing we ain't got much use for around here is the law."

Last summer we were laying off Duck Rock in Bud Kirk's crudely spacious fifty-foot fishing boat, for by now these various Everglades experiences and characters had formed themselves into a story we had begun to film, with Bud as technical adviser. Duck Rock is an Audubon bird sanctuary, one of the great bird-watching sites of the world, where a hundred thousand birds—spoonbills, egrets, blue and white herons, man-of-wars, ibis, anhingas—streak out in incredible formations against the most spectacular sunrises I have ever seen, and return in their mysterious squadrons at dusk, silhouetted against the heartbreaking red and purple western sky. When night fell and the birds had finally settled down to their nightly gossip and prolonged argument, as to just whose branch belonged to whom, Jack Best, the young Duck Rock warden, came over from his small launch to trade his quiet Carolina wit for a few cans of beer and some deckside conversation.

"Don't you get lonely out here by yourself?" somebody asked.

"Lonely?" He shrugged, and his slow smile characteristically lagged several seconds behind his thoughts. "You c'n feel more lonely in Miami. I miss it out here when I have to go back there to our office. Listen to that racket." We all listened to the incessant babble of Duck Rock. "I've got a noisy city of a hundred thousand birds. That should be enough company."

That night I lay in my bunk, listening to the birds we had come to photograph, trying to hide from the mosquitoes, thinking about Jack Best and Bud Kirk, and the time we got lost in the narrow creeks beyond the Little Shark, and the drinking-near-knifing bout with the half-breed Indian, and the continuing war between the bird-and-'gator hunters and the wardens and the fantastic days of the plume hunting when plumes went as high as sixty dollars an ounce; I thought about Bradley and McLeod, the wardens who had given their lives in the feather fight fifty years earlier, simple, unassuming, unheroic men probably not too different from Jack Best here, and I thought about the embattled, no-use-for-lawmen Billy B.'s, enemies of the Park and of the birds, and yet impossible to consider as villains: Somehow they belonged to the Everglades as much as the saw grass and the big cypress, the white herons and the black turkey buzzards.

Out of all these themes and threads and impressions and convictions grew my story of the Everglades. I have tried my best to tell a true story of civilized man versus natural man, pitted against each other in one of the most remote and uncanny regions on this earth.

In the first days of the world's creation it must have been like this. Is it our inevitable tragedy that in our praiseworthy efforts to preserve this wilderness, we must tame or drive out the men who were its natural inhabitants? Perhaps, in order to progress, to conserve, to further the constructive ends of society we must sacrifice some original quality of self-reliance. The Cottonmouths must die. And the Walts, the wardens, whose mission is to destroy these Cottonmouths, weep at their passing.

And the saw grass and the cypress and the mangrove, in the motionless water moving imperceptibly through them and around them, wait for their answer. Having taken their stand in the marsh before the emergence of man, they are willing to wait and wait—and wait, until his kind is gone once more.

ACKNOWLEDGMENTS

Across the Everglades was filmed in the Everglades, with headquarters at Everglades City, from early November, 1957, to late January of 1958. It was a Schulberg Production for Warner Bros., written by the undersigned, produced by Stuart Schulberg, with the direction credited to Nick Ray. Earl Mohn served both as research director and as executive assistant to the producers.

The cast was headed by Burl Ives as Cottonmouth, chieftain of a gang of plume hunters in the Glades, and Christopher Plummer as the Audubon warden sent in to protect the decimated plume birds. Cottonmouth's gang was portrayed by Pat Henning as Sawdust, Tony Galento as Beef, Curt Conway as Perfesser, Sammy Renick as Loser, Emmett Kelly as Bigamy Bob, Fred Grossinger as Slow-Boy, Peter Falk as Writer, Sumner Williams as Windy, Corey Osceola as Billy One-Arm, Brad Bradford as Thumbs. Toch Brown, an Everglades fisherman-bard, struck us as a natural for One-Note. Like Toch, my old fishing and Matusa-rum drinking chum from Key West, Toby Bruce, made his cinematic debut as Joe Bottles. Mary Melons (Dorothy Rogers) and her daughter Memory (Cynthia Bebeau) were little-theatre actresses recruited in Sarasota. Also from Sarasota, from Stu Lancaster's Palm Tree Playhouse, in addition to Grossinger, came Frank Rothe as Ross Morgan, Mary Pennington as Mrs. Liggett, and Owen Pavitt as the Sheriff.

Representing early Miami in our story were Gypsy Rose Lee as Mrs. Bradford, George Voskovec as Aaron Nathanson, Howard Smith as George Liggett, Chana Eden as Naomi Nathanson and Pulitzer-prize-winning author MacKinlay Kantor, stealing time off from a forthcoming novel to play Judge Tippins. Our ragtime piano player and blues singer at Mrs. Bradford's is Rufus Beecham.

Joseph Brun, who did marvels with an inexplicably overcast winter, was our director of cinematography. Assistant director was Charles Maguire, with whom I had worked on *Waterfront* and *A Face in the Crowd*. When Nick Ray was forced to withdraw because of illness, Maguire, Mr. Brun and I worked harmoniously together to guide our vessel through tropical storms and safely into port.

Our art director, who made early Miami come alive before our eyes, was Dick Sylbert. And Frank Thompson's costumes were equally effective in recapturing the atmosphere of fifty years ago.

Riding our Mitchell again as camera operator was Sol Midwall. "Fearless" Jimmy Dillinger, our gaffer or chief electrician, also served as impromptu head life-saver, fishing out the director, the assistant director and numerous others who went into the drink in the course of a production that called for a maximum amount of "sea duty."

George (old Keep 'Em in the East) Justin was production manager; Bud Kirk, described at some length in the introduction, served as technical adviser. Ernest Zatorsky was in charge of sound. The script girl, once again, was Roberta Hodes. The intricacies of make-up, in which an actor sometimes had to change from paleface to sunburn to tan and back to paleface in a single day, were in the sensitive hands of Bob Jiras. Our creative film editors were George Klotz and Joseph Zigman. The auditors, who somehow kept track of the money it cost us to move a not-so-small army into the Everglades for three months, were "Dutch" Myer and Augie Joos. Mr. Hugh Parker, secretary of

ACKNOWLEDGMENTS

the Everglades City Chamber of Commerce, doubled as liaison officer and part-time actor.

Our film could not have been made without the co-operation of the Collier Corporation, headed by Barron Collier. Its chief executive, Norman Herren, not only opened innumerable doors for us but provided many invaluable services, even personally conducting us on a memorable wading tour to Deep Lake, that led us to our final location, the cypress swamp which was both forbidding and beautiful, exactly as the Glades are supposed to be. Our entire company was grateful to Mr. Herren and his associates for their assistance and hospitality throughout our stay.

We are equally grateful to the National Audubon Society, to its New York headquarters and to Charles Brookfield and Jack Best in the field, both for checking our story for authenticity and for permitting us to photograph their bird sanctuaries, often from closer angles than these unusual birds have ever been photographed before.

We are also indebted to Dr. Ken Snyder and his nurse Gretchen Gerish, to Mildred Cook of the Bank of Everglades, to the Rod & Gun Club, with especially fond memories of bartender Andy and bellboy-diplomat Freddie, and to Bob Longmire, custodian of the venerable movie house, who graciously projected our rushes.

Across the Everglades is to be released in the fall of 1958 by Warner Bros., whose chief executives, Jack Warner and Ben Kalmenson, and their staffs, deserve our thanks for their unqualified support of our undertaking.

B. S.

AUTHOR'S NOTE

Except for establishing the change of scene, the specified camera angles—which may number as many as four or five hundred in a detailed shooting script—have been eliminated from this edition. What remains is the complete text, full dialogue, stage directions, scene and mood descriptions, exactly as photographed and recorded. Inevitably in the editing of this film material, certain deletions or adjustments are made in the interest of pace and cinematic unity. The author believes that while the inclusion and enumeration of the technical shots would be of interest to the student of the cinema, to delineate the shots would interrupt the narrative flow for the general reader. An absence of technical terms and jargon will allow the reader to experience the drama on the printed page in the same way that the film audience experiences the motion picture —as a continuously unfolding plot and theme.

ACROSS THE EVERGLADES

A Play for the Screen

In the early 1900's the plumes of tropical birds adorned most ladies' hats. More than fashion, it was a craze that swept the world. Plumes rose in value until an ounce of feathers was worth two ounces of gold. America's plume birds were being sacrificed to "the senseless demands of fashion," as increasingly aroused nature lovers charged. To save the snowy egrets, blue herons and other rare birds from total extinction, a small, embattled Audubon Society waged a two-front war, fighting for laws that would ban the plume traffic and recruiting wardens, commissioned as Florida State Marshals, to establish bird sanctuaries and to apprehend the plume gangs who were plundering the unexplored water wilderness of the Everglades.

FADE IN: 1905. MIAMI R.R. STATION—DAY

A sunny afternoon. The arrival of a train in Miami is still the great event of the week and there is a holiday spirit in the crowd, some 200 people, including Seminole Indians and a dozen or so small children—a few with their ears to the track waiting to catch the first sound of the approaching engine. There are also hound dogs, puppies, four or five chickens, oblivious of the crowd, and a cow, indicating the rural, even primitive, character of frontier Miami. On the Miami River, near its mouth at Biscayne Bay, we see sailing vessels tied up to the dock, with some under way in the river. At the end of the track is a sign—a landmark of its time—which reads: MIAMI, U.S.A., ENTRANCE TO FAIRYLAND. Beyond lies tropical wilderness.

In the background, leading from the station into town, is a row of one- and two-story buildings. There are horses and carriages, three or four vintage motorcars and old bicycles.

Unofficially presiding over this quaint gathering of turn-of-the-century Miamians is JUDGE TIPPINS, *a distinguished-looking gentleman in a frock coat and top hat. His spirit is that of aristocratic congeniality—something of a poppinjay, a friend to all.*

JUDGE TIPPINS

Mr. Liggett, good day to you, sir.

*On the platform of his warehouse—in front of a sign advertising GEO. LIGGETT & CO.—*LIGGETT, *a florid, fleshy, bewhiskered, amiable man, bows. He has just* *chased some children away from his resplendent "new" Cadillac.*

LIGGETT

Judge Tippins. (*To the children*) What you doing on that Cadillac? Get away from there!

JUDGE TIPPINS

(*Doffing his hat in another direction, to a handsome lady in her mid-forties—this is* MRS. BRADFORD)

Lovely afternoon, **madame**.

MRS. BRADFORD, *who affects a honey-sweet Southern accent and extreme gentility, bows graciously, acknowledging the* JUDGE, *who moves on, bowing and tipping his hat to one and all.*

JUDGE TIPPINS

Mr. Nathanson and Miss Naomi! How are you? Another grand day for the arrival of our train.

AARON NATHANSON, *a pioneer Miami storekeeper, a robust, deeply tanned, middle-aged man, full of irrepressible energy and good humor, nods. With him is his daughter,* NAOMI, *a dark, handsome, high-spirited girl.*

NATHANSON

A jewel of a day, Judge. South Florida!

The train's warning whistle sets off a Breughel-like chain reaction: mothers grabbing their children off the track, a boy retrieving a pet fox, chickens and dogs scattering to get out of the way. NAOMI *hurries off on her high-wheel bicycle to get a better view of the train.*

A wood-burning engine of the period, pulling two or more coaches, a baggage car, a flat car and a caboose, chugs into view.

ACROSS THE EVERGLADES

Leaning his head out of the wooden coach is WALT MURDOCK, *a twenty-seven-year old naturalist, sturdily built, whose nature combines physical rebellion and a scholarly, even poetic, turn of mind. He peers through the smoke for his first glimpse of Miami.*

He takes in the colorful surroundings, the palm trees, the horse-and-buggies, a few horseless carriages, *the Seminoles in their brilliant shirts and turbans, the charming-looking ladies with their parasols and ankle-length dresses, the riverfront roughnecks; the hustle-and-bustle of this frontier town in the American tropics.*

As he draws his head back into the car we see behind him four attractive girls wearing an abundance of egret feathers on their hats, for elaborate plumes and even whole birds are the millinery fashion of the day. He eyes their display with distaste.

On the coach platform, as WALT *steps aside for the four young ladies to descend, the stylish plumes of their hats literally brush his nose. He glares at the offending plumes.*

As the young ladies approach the platform they are greeted by MRS. BRADFORD, *whose hat represents a small rookery.*

MRS. BRADFORD
(To one of the young ladies who is sporting a black eye)
Hello, Miss Sally, I see you had a nice weekend. *(To another girl, this one a tall beauty)* You must be Miss Denise. Welcome to ah fair city; ah hope you young ladies ah goin' t'be mahty happy at mah establishment.

MISS DENISE
(With northern nasality)
I'm sure I will.

3

MRS. BRADFORD

I'm from Jersey City myself but we're in the South now and I think a southern accent is much more refined—don't you?

MISS DENISE
(*Catching on*)

Ah certainly do!

As MRS. BRADFORD *gathers her young ladies together,* WALT MURDOCK *watches amusedly. Then, remembering his purpose in Miami, he turns to the* SHERIFF, *who has been overseeing the arrival.*

WALT

Have you seen the high school principal? (*Then, as* MRS. BRADFORD'*s ladies brush by*) What's she running—some kind of young ladies' finishing school?

SHERIFF

Mrs. Bradford's? I heard it called just about everything but I ain't never heard it called that before. It's in North Miami—out of my jurisdiction.

Descending just behind WALT *is a lady of forty, a rather different type from the four attractive and showy girls reporting to* MRS. BRADFORD. *This woman,* MRS. LIGGETT, *like the others, wears a hat decorated with egret feathers. She seems to be something of a personage in town, for the porter treats her differently from the others.*

PORTER

Let me help you down with your bags, Mrs. Liggett, ma'am.

On his warehouse platform, LIGGETT, *attended by a slight, foppishly dressed Englishman, is supervising the delivery of a shipment of plumes. The two men making the delivery are a couple of disreputable, even piratical-looking characters, dirtier, more ragged and unshaven than the frontier people they move among. One wears a pair of steel-rimmed glasses that gives him an oddly intellectual look, the other is gaunt, tense, somewhat evil-looking, with a thumb missing from his left hand.*

LIGGETT

(*To English assistant as he studies the plumes which are carefully pressed between the pages of a large book*)

Take 'em inside 'n count 'em. 'N don't pay 'em off till you make sure every one of those feathers is in perfect condition.

ASSISTANT

(*Fawning*)

Very good, Mr. Liggett.

MRS. LIGGETT *hurries across the platform to join her husband. One of the longer feathers on her hat brushes* WALT'S *face as he stands near her waiting for his luggage. With an impetuous gesture,* WALT *pulls the offending feather out of her hat.*

MRS. LIGGETT

(*Outraged*)

What are you doing to my hat?

WALT

(*With an impulsiveness born of deep conviction*)

Madame, how would you like it if this bird wore you for a decoration?

MRS. LIGGETT

(*Screaming*)

George! George! That man tore . . .

MR. LIGGETT *comes blustering down the warehouse*

5

steps, followed by THUMBS *and* PERFESSER. *Calling the*
SHERIFF, *he and his men grab the astonished* WALT.

WALT

Look—I'm giving her back her feather. When these Indians
wear feathers on their hats we call them savages. But we think
we're civilized.

MRS. LIGGETT

Oh, this is an outrage. How dare you, how dare you!

LIGGETT

One more word out of you and I'll take a horsewhip to you,
I'll— Sheriff! Sheriff, arrest this man.

While THUMBS *and* PERFESSER *scurry off to their skiff
on the other side of the train, the* SHERIFF *moves in on*
WALT.

SHERIFF

I'll handle this. Who are you? What's your name?

WALT

The name's Murdock. I've come down here to teach Nature
Studies in the new high school.

LIGGETT

As a member of our school board, let me tell you you'll never
get closer to the high school than you are right now.

SHERIFF

Want me to lock him up, Mr. Liggett?

LIGGETT

Yes, Clyde.

SHERIFF

I'll hold him for Judge Tippins in the morning. Okay, Judge?

JUDGE TIPPINS *is on the train platform helping down
some ladies.*

JUDGE TIPPINS

Indeed, yes, Sheriff. (*To a lady*) Come, my dear.

Further down the station platform, J. ROSS MORGAN *watches* WALT *being led away.* MORGAN *is an aristocratic-looking man of fifty, nicely dressed in yachting clothes of the day, sunburned but suggesting some frailty, and carrying a walking stick with which he tries to conceal a rather extreme limp in his right leg.* MORGAN *watches* WALT *with unusual interest. Standing with* MORGAN *is his friend* AARON NATHANSON. NAOMI *returns to them on her bicycle.*

MORGAN

There's an interesting young fellow.

NAOMI

Poppa, Poppa, the player piano isn't on the train. Nine weeks ago they promised to send it and—

NATHANSON

(*Philosophically*)

So maybe it will be on next week's train. I say all things come to Miami—if only you have the patience to wait that long, my impatient daughter Naomi.

MORGAN *smiles but is still preoccupied with* WALT's *demonstration.*

MORGAN

(*Smiling slightly*)

You know, Aaron, for years I've had an impulse to yank that feather off Mrs. Liggett's hat.

NAOMI

Now, Ross, don't you get into any trouble.

NATHANSON *and* NAOMI *take leave of* MORGAN, *who starts in the opposite direction, following the* SHERIFF *and* WALT.

INTERIOR JUDGE TIPPINS' CHAMBER—DAY

> *This is a small, unpretentious room to the rear of the* JUDGE's *courtroom. There is a battered sofa, with the stuffing bleeding out of it, a roll-top desk and period desk chair and some Civil War pictures. The* JUDGE *is a Civil War veteran, distinguished-looking in a some-what deteriorated way. He is an easygoing figure of pomp and circumstance, a pillar of society—albeit a slightly leaning pillar. He is far from a drunkard, but he may take a nip or two of sour-mash by way of tonic. With him is* ROSS MORGAN. WALT *is led into the chamber by the* JAILER.

JAILER

Judge Tippins—here's the fellow you asked for.

JUDGE TIPPINS

Sit down, young fellow. It may seem irregular for you to be summoned out of your cell for a personal talk, but we're an informal, easygoing town and I've found that sometimes justice is better served through a private office than a public court.

WALT

Whatever the reason, it's good to be out of that cell. Cooped up! I hate that feeling. That's why I left New York.

JUDGE TIPPINS

I've called you in as a favor to an old friend of mine—(*Bows to* MORGAN)—Ross Morgan. You've heard of the Audubon Society?

WALT

Of course, I was a biology teacher.

JUDGE TIPPINS

Mr. Morgan is head of the local chapter.

ACROSS THE EVERGLADES

WALT

Ross Morgan. You wrote some books.

MORGAN

A few.

WALT

The Vanishing Birds.

MORGAN

That was one.

WALT

And *Last Wilderness*—that trip you took through the Glades.

MORGAN

The Glades. Yes, I've been in the Glades. (*Taps his leg significantly*) In fact, that brings me to what I came here for.

JUDGE TIPPINS

(*Getting up and crossing to the mirror*)

Gentlemen, I hope you'll forgive me if I give myself a trim while you continue your interview. (*Admiring himself in the mirror*) The shape of one's beard—like the furtherance of justice—must follow a traditional form, allowing of no loose ends. (*Nipping off a tuft of beard*)

MORGAN

Before I explain—may I ask a few questions?

WALT

Anything is better than pacing that cell.

MORGAN

Where are you from?

WALT

Buffalo.

MORGAN

What brings you down here?

9

WALT

I was teaching in a finishing school. One day I found my-self giving a lecture on conservation to a bunch of feather-brained girls, whispering, giggling, and passing notes about the Saturday tea-dance. I walked out of the classroom—and—here I am. . . .

The JAILER *enters and stands respectfully in the door-way.*

JAILER

Your Honor, your luncheon at the Ladies' League for Civic Betterment is starting in twenty minutes.

JUDGE TIPPINS

Well, thank you. Speech—speech—(*He looks around room, then takes a sheaf of papers out of cubbyhole in desk*) Ah, here—one of my better ones. I'll give them this. Gentlemen, why don't you walk along with me to the hotel? (*To* JAILER) It's all right, Joe, I'll be responsible for him.

WALT

I promise not to escape without permission.

They start out.

DISSOLVE

EXTERIOR MIAMI COURTHOUSE

The JUDGE, MORGAN *and* WALT *are walking through a tropical formal garden, bordering the riverfront, on their way to the Greek-Southern hotel manse.*

MORGAN

This feather craze—if it keeps on, there won't be a plume bird—an egret—a roseate spoonbill—left in America. The State is too poor to employ wardens to protect our birds. So we Audubon people have been trying to fill the gap, sending men into the Glades to locate and protect the rookeries.

WALT

Mmm-hmmm.

MORGAN

Any idea what you do now?

WALT

I'm young. I've got my health. I've got a couple of dollars saved up. Maybe I'll ship out to California. Or even Alaska.

MORGAN

(*With a long, searching look*)
You know, you may be the man I'm looking for.

WALT

(*Studying* MORGAN *a moment*)
I'd do almost anything to stay out of that jail.

JUDGE TIPPINS

Son, before you accept your freedom under Mr. Morgan's conditions, I think you ought to know you would be entering the most lawless territory left in America.

WALT

I'm all for saving those birds—but to tell the truth, Mr. Morgan, I'm not sure I'm brave enough for that.

MORGAN

I'm not sure I'm brave enough to send you. We're not only against killing off birds. We're even for conserving biology teachers.

WALT *smiles.*

JUDGE TIPPINS

(*Stopping for a moment behind some tropical foliage and drinking from flask*)
Gentlemen, excuse me, got to fortify myself before I face those women-folk.

WALT

If I take this job, I'm a free man? Even if I don't like it and quit, I'm still free?

JUDGE TIPPINS

After all, it was more of a prank than a deliberate crime. We're a small town. I'm sure I can get the Liggetts to drop the charges.

WALT

Okay, I'll try it. If I don't like it, I'll move on.

MORGAN

(*Smiling*)

You know, maybe you've got to be a cigar-smoking, strong-language hot-head to face the Everglades.

JUDGE TIPPINS

Young man, your sentence is officially commuted to a wardenship in the Audubon Society. Good luck and good day, gentlemen.

JUDGE TIPPINS *enters the hotel with his typical judicial flourish.*

MORGAN

Come along, let's collect your things and I'll help you get settled.

MORGAN *and* WALT *walk off together, along the Miami riverfront.*

DISSOLVE

NATHANSON STORE—LATER THAT DAY—EXTERIOR

MORGAN *leads* WALT *up the weather-beaten stairs to the balcony of the faded-red, sprawling, homemade, two-story store perched on the seasoned dock overlooking the bay. This general store, serving townspeople, Indians, fishermen and trappers, is a frontier landmark.*

MORGAN

Our big hotels are a little too much for an Audubon budget, but Aaron Nathanson has a couple of rooms he lets out here in his store—the first one in town—practically saved our lives.

WALT

(*Observing the weather-beaten wood, the picturesque architecture, the commanding location on the bay*)

I think I like it already.

Their attention is drawn to raucous singing on the bay. There they see THUMBS *and* PERFESSER *passing close to shore in their boat. They glance malevolently over their shoulders at* MORGAN *and* WALT. *The* PERFESSER *is teetering unsteadily in the boat, holding onto a jug with one hand and onto* THUMBS *with another, improvising a song: "When you go to* MRS. BRADFORD's, *hide your money in your shoes . . ."*

WALT

Aren't those the two lovelies who roughed me up at the station this morning?

MORGAN

The one who looks like a pirate—all muscles and veins— that's Thumbs. His left hand happens to lack that particular digit. The other is called Perfesser. Apparently he's spent a good deal of his time in the library—of the State prison.

WALT

You seem to know them pretty well.

MORGAN

I should—they're two of Cottonmouth's boys.

WALT

Cottonmouth?

13

MORGAN

The leader of a band of swamp rats—has his headquarters seventy miles across the Glades in Lostman's River. Only man I ever heard of carries a cottonmouth snake in his pocket— they're more poisonous than rattlers and they don't do you the courtesy of announcing themselves.

WALT

So that's why they call him Cottonmouth?

MORGAN

There's another reason—he's soft-spoken, deceptive, sneaks up on you and then he strikes, like the cottonmouth.

WALT

Sounds like quite a fellow.

MORGAN

I was at the head of Lostman's River with a warrant for him when I got this—(*Taps leg*). By the time the guide got me out my leg was as big as that piling. So now I'm a sideline soldier. Come in and meet the Nathansons.

EXTERIOR BAY—DAY

Close on THUMBS *and* PERFESSER, *their boat under way.*

THUMBS

Looks like the Audubon fella found himself a new bird-boy.

PERFESSER

As the spider said to the fly, so the Glades say to the Audubon, "Won't you come into my parlor?"

He breaks into drunken song again, as THUMBS *rows on.*

INTERIOR NATHANSON STORE—DAY

The inside of the store is even more unusual than it seemed from the outside. It presents an ingenious clutter of kitchen utensils, hunting and fishing equipment, hides, furs, books, clothing, pails, lanterns, strewn along a dark-paneled, inviting, tunnel-like room, one side of which serves the Nathansons as living quarters that combine an old-world Jewish atmosphere with frontier trading-post effects. NATHANSON *comes from the back of the store where* NAOMI *is waiting on several customers.* WALT *puts down his suitcase.*

MORGAN

Aaron, here's your new boarder, Walt Murdock. I'm sure you'll find him very quiet and well-behaved for a jailbird.

NATHANSON

Fortunately my daughter doesn't believe in wearing feathers on her hats. Well, young man, how do you like our metropolis? Wonderful climate! Wonderful people! Come and have some tea.

NATHANSON *leads* WALT *and* MORGAN *into a small alcove that serves as kitchen and dining room. From a kettle on the stove he pours some hot tea for them.*

MORGAN

Aaron is one of our earliest and most enthusiastic settlers. Came here when there were only five hundred people.

NATHANSON

(*Proudly*)

Most of them living in tents and palmetto shacks.

WALT

(*Looking around in wonder at the motley articles*)

I've never seen such a store.

NATHANSON

Our motto has always been—if you need anything, just ask for it—and if we don't have it, we'll show you how to get along without it.

MORGAN

Aaron is interested in the Glades too—in a different way.

NATHANSON
(*Launching enthusiastically*)

You see, my idea for the Glades is drainage—a State franchise to cut canals. . . .

> NAOMI *hurries up and puts out her hand to* WALT *with characteristic directness.*

NAOMI

Hello, I'm Naomi.

MORGAN

Miss Nathanson—Mr. Murdock. As you see, I leave you in good hands. I'll be back in the morning to help you line up your equipment. Aaron. Miss Naomi.

He bows and leaves.

WALT

How did you two ever get this far—from wherever you started?

NATHANSON

After her mother died in Dunaberg, we dreamed of a new country—America—fresh air—fresh opportunity—

NAOMI

New York, the East Side—little rooms, crowded streets—wasn't what we pictured at all.

NATHANSON
(*Chuckling*)

I wanted to find "wide-open spaces"—"ride 'em, cowboy"—like I read about in your dime novels.

NAOMI
(*Smiling*)

Poppa loves the cowboy movies at the nickelodeon.

NATHANSON

My favorite is "Broncho Billy." You know, one thing I like about this country right away—if you don't like one place, so you move to another. In the old country you need a passport to cross the street. Here your only passport is the carfare.

NAOMI

One day we read in the papers about a place we never even heard of—Florida.

NATHANSON

We took all our savings down to the railroad station and pushed them through the little hole of the ticket booth. "Will this take us to Florida?" I said. "Pal," he says to me—he doesn't even know me and already he's calling me *pal*—"this will take you all the way to Miami." "Miami, what kind of name is Miami? Maybe there are wild Indians, savages there," I said to Naomi.

NAOMI

And I said, "Poppa, I like the name. We'll go to Miami."

NATHANSON

(*Exuberantly*)

We were on the third train into Miami. After tipping the porter we had seventy-five cents left.

WALT

It takes courage.

NATHANSON

(*Shrugging—half laughing*)

Courage? What's so special to a people who survived Egypt and Rome and the Middle Ages? Anyway, I love it here—I swim every morning before breakfast. After lunch I lie half an hour in the sun. I feel I belong here—part of South Florida

17

—a frontier. And out there—beyond the river—a wilderness waits to be developed—to be—

A bell clangs loudly.

NATHANSON
(*Breaking off*)
Excuse me—a last-minute customer. Okay, okay, I'm coming, I'm coming.

NAOMI
Just in time. His drainage speech was coming on again. Come, I'll show you to your room.

As he follows her with his luggage.

QUICK DISSOLVE

INTERIOR WALT'S BEDROOM—NATHANSON ROOMING HOUSE

As NAOMI *leads* WALT *in. It is a small, unadorned room with a brass bed.*

NAOMI
Here are towels, soap, and fresh water from the cistern. You are lucky. We had a good rain last night.

WALT *immediately starts to wash himself, pouring water from the large pitcher into the porcelain washbowl.*

WALT
What this town needs is a larger, cleaner jail.

NAOMI
(*She takes out a cigarette*)
You mind if I smoke a cigarette?

WALT
(*Looking up from the washbasin*)
I never saw a girl smoke before.

NAOMI
European women do. I believe in doing what I feel like doing. I think American girls are afraid to be themselves.

18

WALT

They're so busy being young ladies. Pampered Victorians. I don't mind if you smoke. If you enjoy it, why not? I'm a cigar-smoker myself.

NAOMI

I'll bring you some. Poppa gets very good ones from Key West.

WALT

Don't go. Er—help me unpack. I'll have plenty of time to be alone.

> *Both of them begin to unpack his suitcase.* WALT *puts his shirts in the dresser, hangs up his coat jackets, etc.*

NAOMI

Are you really going to take the river into the Glades?

WALT

That's what I promised Mr. Morgan.

NAOMI

Have people told you how dangerous it is?

WALT

I'm beginning to get the idea.

NAOMI

What made you take such a job?

WALT

I don't know. I lost the job I came down here for anyway. And I was feeling restless, fed up with cities and the way people run around chasing their tails in selfish little circles. And I guess somebody has to save those birds from being wiped out. As Mr. Morgan says, set up a sanctuary.

NAOMI

I know what you mean. It's a terrible thing to be hunted down. People need sanctuaries too. Poppa and I knew that fear once. Here we're not afraid any more. Poppa is proud. He's a leading citizen. We found our place.

They look at each other. There is a moment of under-standing, of mutual sympathy, between them.

NAOMI

(*Embarrassed*)

If—if there's anything you want, lanterns, fishing tackle, sun helmets—we sell that downstairs. They serve food up the street where it says EATS. Such a funny American word. And we're proud of our new ice-cream parlor and our new theater, Kelly's Nickelodeon.

WALT

How about whiskey?

NAOMI

Just outside the town limits there's a gambling hall—Mrs. Bradford's—she also runs an elegant saloon. Everything is elegant at Mrs. Bradford's except for the sidewalk saloon she runs for the sailors and swamp angels. If they don't have three murders between midnight and dawn it's a quiet night.

WALT

At least you seem to have plenty of girls in this town.

NAOMI

(*Amused*)

You Americans seem to want everything in quantities—cigars fifty to a box—

WALT

I didn't mean to make it sound like a smoke.

NAOMI

You don't have to explain.

WALT

I guess not. After all, you smoke.

NAOMI

You see, you're not so far from the Victorians yourself. If a girl smokes cigarettes, she must be a scarlet woman. (*Then, more seriously*) Actually, nothing shocks me. We've come a long way. I've seen a little of everything.

WALT

You know, I don't think I ever knew a . . . European girl before. You have such a new world face—(*Grins*)—and such an old world mind.

NAOMI

If you're looking for girls, Mrs. Bradford takes great pride in her hostesses. Those were her "Nieces" getting off the train with you.

Suddenly, from below the window comes an eerie cry.

GUTTURAL VOICE

Nakuni naknosi—

WALT

(*Going to the window, alarmed*)

What the devil is that?

Looking down into the street below, WALT *and* NAOMI *see an extremely tall Seminole,* SAM TIGERTAIL, *in exotic dress, holding up two kittens and chanting in Seminole.*

NAOMI

That's only Sam Tigertail—when he drinks a little too much whyome—that's Seminole for moonshine—Poppa lets him sleep it off at the back of the store.

WALT

He sounds wild. Is he—perfectly safe?

NAOMI

(*Gently mocking*)

My goodness, if you're going to be frightened by a Seminole

hunter like Sam Tigertail who brings in our otter skins every week, what's going to happen to you in the Glades?

WALT

I read everything I could find on the Seminoles. That's the first time I ever heard of an Indian pitching a chikee in the back of a general store.

NAOMI

This place is full of surprises.

WALT

I'm beginning to see that.

NAOMI *crosses to the door of the bedroom.*

NAOMI

(*Abruptly*)

Meals come with the room. Supper's at six.

She is gone. WALT *looks after her, interested, moved. Then the cry of a bird draws his attention to the river and he watches as hundreds of them fly by, seeming to beckon him into the Glades.*

DISSOLVE

EXTERIOR MIAMI DOCK—DAWN

WALT *is in his canvas canoe, loaded with his equipment and supplies: rifle, mosquito bar, lantern, folding tent, box camera, etc. He wears his pants tucked into his leggings, an outer jacket for protection—the motif of a greenhorn over-uniformed for his mission.* MORGAN *is with him.*

MORGAN

Here's a chart I made of the route to Chikikee Rookery. It's about twenty-five miles. Don't try going any farther this trip. Good luck.

WALT

Thank you, sir.

MORGAN

All I can say is, I envy you.

> MORGAN *withdraws as* NAOMI *runs in, and hurries to him in the half-light.*

NAOMI

I brought you some coffee—(*Hands him an early-type thermos*)—and some Key West cigars—and a flask of Cuban rum.

WALT

Coffee, cigars, rum—I may never come back.

NAOMI

Have you a very good imagination?

WALT

(*Surprised*)

I think so—why?

NAOMI

Keep imagining the worst things that can happen to you. What people call courage—it's mostly the failure of the imagination.

WALT

I never heard it called that before.

NAOMI

When are you coming back?

WALT

Sometime tomorrow. I just want to get the feel of it, camp out one night and come back in. I won't be looking for Cottonmouth—not yet.

NAOMI

He may be looking for you.

> WALT *looks at her thoughtfully and then pushes off from the dock.* NATHANSON *joins* NAOMI *on the dock,*

23

throwing a coat over her shoulders. NATHANSON, NAOMI
and MORGAN *watch* WALT *as he heads down the river,
into the tropical unknown. He turns and waves, then
disappears around a mangrove key with the first rays
of sunrise behind him.*

DISSOLVE

SOME MILES UP THE MIAMI RIVER—MORNING

WALT *passes through some rapids into calm, sparkling
water. Beyond the banks the terrain has begun to take
on the character of the Everglades—great stretches of
saw grass punctuated by thickly wooded hammocks. In
the opposite direction a battered thirty-foot sloop approaches, skippered by a scrawny cracker with a big
rum-blossom nose on a weathered squint-eyed face. This
is* JOE BOTTLES. WALT *stops his canoe alongside the sloop.*

JOE BOTTLES

Goin' huntin', stranger?

WALT

Something like that.

JOE BOTTLES

They call me Joe Bottles. I peddle shine along the river and
down through the Keys. Wanna buy a jug?

WALT

Is it any good?

JOE BOTTLES

Any good? Why, friend, I drink this here bush-lightning
myself.

He does so.

WALT

Okay, I'll try it. If I don't like it, I'll return the bottle.

JOE BOTTLES

(*Handing over the jug*)

What yuh don't drink yuh c'n rub on yer arms t'kill the swamp hussies.

WALT

Swamp what?

JOE BOTTLES

Skeeters. I call 'em swamp hussies 'cuz its oney the lady that bites yuh. So all ya gotta do is tell the boy skeeters from the gal skeeters an' ya know which ones t'duck. (*Puts hand out*) That'll be one buck—mainline.

WALT

Main what?

JOE BOTTLES

Ya ain't been around long, have yuh? That's cracker lingo fer hard cash. (*As he pockets* WALT's *bill*) Thanks—I'd get home afore dark if I was you.

WALT

Because of your swamp hussies?

JOE BOTTLES

Man, they got a little of everything in there.

He gives WALT *a little farewell salute as* WALT *paddles off into the Glades.*

DISSOLVE

FURTHER INTO THE GLADES—DAY

Rounding a bend in the river, bordered with coconut and cabbage palms, WALT *comes upon a group of live oaks festooned with wild orchids. Pausing to take in the strange beauty of the outer Glades, he notices a pair of pileated woodpeckers drilling away at a royal palm. Then a squadron of swallow-tailed kites come darting by. One sees a fish, dives and comes up with it.* WALT *enjoys the sights and paddles on. The canals or creeks begin to fork off from one another, the almost hidden water paths fanning out like lines in a hand. As Walt turns down one canal, his canoe comes face to face with an alligator slithering down a bank.* WALT *takes a good look at it and paddles on.*

He begins to see more birds, various small herons, white ibis, great blue and white herons, the startling black-headed wood ibis, all flying in the same direction. As he reaches the shallows he sees a few roseate spoonbills wading with stiff-legged dignity, sifting their food with the curious sidewise motion of their flattened spoonlike bills. Suddenly there is a great flurry overhead and he sees for the first time a great white cloud of snowy egrets flying to their rookery on a water-surrounded hammock. Carefully WALT *edges his canoe into the bank and stealthily climbs ashore, carrying his camera.*

CHIKIKEE HAMMOCK

As WALT *finishes setting up his camera and looks into it under the hood, we have the visual effect of egrets being brought into focus, when suddenly he sees upside-down in his lens an unexpected object: A red-bearded giant whose powerful, broad-jawed, wilderness-toughened face is crowned by a flamboyant gaucho hat set off by a snowy white feather. This man—to be known as Cottonmouth—wears a huge, worn hunting jacket and much lived-in yellow-green trousers tucked into weathered yellow-brown great-boots. There is a wild, yet regal, authority about him as he stands there holding a machete and a thick, yard-long cabbage palm—his sword and scepter. Under the hood of the camera* WALT *waves the formidable stranger away. But the man doesn't move.* WALT *comes out from under the hood.*

STRANGER

Gettin' some pretty pictures?

WALT

(*Startled*)

Where did you come from?

STRANGER

(*Mischievously gentle*)

I ask the questions around here. (*With his machete, he lops off a piece of the cabbage palm and chews on it*) Swamp cabbage. Keeps yer belly healthy. (*Tossing a chunk to* WALT) Here, have a chaw.

WALT

Thanks. You got a place around here?

STRANGER

I got a thousand places around here. Every spot of high ground 'tween here 'n Cape Sable. I was born in here 'n when I'm three score and ten, I'll die here with the seeds of a cabbage palm in my guts so's a tree'll grow out 'n stand on top o' me.

His hearty laugh, his lusty acceptance of this natural life, rings through the trees. WALT *can't help being attracted to the wild naturalness of this man. He joins in the laughter. Startled, great numbers of birds rise in a fluttering circle overhead.*

WALT

We're scaring the birds.

STRANGER

They'll be back. They're nestin' here now. I can show you where there's more of 'em.

WALT *stoops to pick up his camera and equipment. As he looks up again, the stranger has disappeared noiselessly into the brush like a snake.* WALT *looks after him,*

*disconcerted and yet unaccountably attracted to this
strange, monumental figure who moves through the
Glades with an animal grace—a wilderness agility. Then
he turns back to his observation of egrets. It is a moment
of white-plumed beauty that* WALT *will always remember.
Then from his knapsack he takes a large sign and begins
to fasten it to the largest tree at the entrance of the clearing. It reads:*

*EVERGLADES AUDUBON ROOKERY NO. 1
KILLING OF BIRDS PROHIBITED BY
FLORIDA STATE LAW
PENALTY: $500 FINE AND/OR SIX MONTHS
IMPRISONMENT*

As WALT *steps back to look at this placard, a thunder-
ous barrage of shotgun fire from unseen guns drowns out
the sounds of birds. Startled,* WALT *runs forward and
sees—*

—Wounded egrets plunging from branches.

*—Bloodied egrets flopping into the shallows they have
been quietly fishing.*

—Close shots of squatters, featuring COTTONMOUTH,
*shouting in hoarse, bull-voiced triumph as birds by
the hundreds fall victim to the shotguns.*

*—The plume hunters, a dozen unwashed, unshaven men
in rough, mud-encrusted clothing, following wounded
birds into the mangrove bush and clubbing them to
death.*

WALT *is sickened as he watches the carnage from con-
cealment. The cries of the birds mingle with the blood-
lusting voices of the hunters.*

COTTONMOUTH *is a commanding figure astride his long,*

red skiff, directing the activities of his men. He is accompanied by his young, dull-witted son, SLOW-BOY.

A PLUME HUNTER

Ya hee! What a haul! North Miami, here we come!

COTTONMOUTH

Stick to business. Don't spare a stinkin' bird. 'N treat them feathers careful. You boys like money! Every bird's a ten-dollar bill. Them Yankees up yonder love the tickle of these feathers jest like we love the tickle o' their money!

WALT *continues to watch as the water reddens with the blood of slaughtered birds.*

Under COTTONMOUTH'S *urging, the plume hunters do a thorough job of wiping out the rookery. Their hands, clothes, even their faces, are smeared or streaked with blood. Their grim work finished as suddenly as it began, they haul their plunder into their boats.*

WALT *stands on the bank of the small lagoon and looks across at* COTTONMOUTH *and his men.* COTTONMOUTH *plays with a pet snake as he calls back confidently:*

COTTONMOUTH

Hey, Audubon, gonna arrest me?

WALT

If you knew what I came in for, why didn't you kill me?

COTTONMOUTH

Too much trouble.

WALT

So you're Cottonmouth.

COTTONMOUTH

The same.

WALT

Those birds are protected by law. I'm going to do my damndest to enforce that law.

COTTONMOUTH

Ya got the badge.

The boys jeer and laugh at WALT. *It's* COTTONMOUTH's *joke.*

A PLUME HUNTER

Go home, Bird-Boy.

Others chime in. COTTONMOUTH *and his group, in their half-dozen boats, turn and head away from the ravaged, silenced rookery. Disturbed, frustrated,* WALT *watches them go.* COTTONMOUTH *and the others can be heard laughing and singing as they pole away. Torn between anger and resignation,* WALT *turns and picks his way through the marshy undergrowth toward his boat.*

DISSOLVE

CLEARING AT COTTONMOUTH KEY—DAY

This is a secluded mangrove key in Lostman's River, one of the great rivers running from the Glades into the Gulf of Mexico. Circling the clearing are a number of makeshift shacks built on buttonwood stilts to accommodate the rising tides that inundate the island shore. A network of precarious catwalks connects the shacks, which are dominated by COTTONMOUTH's. *This larger, more substantial shack has a broad porch from which* COTTONMOUTH, *in his throne-like chair draped with a black bear hide, can preside over the activities of this ragtail community.*

Returned from the rookery and resting from their bloody labors, COTTONMOUTH's *boys are enjoying the homemade music of* ONE-NOTE, *an easygoing cracker cut-throat who is "pickin' 'n singin'" a local ballad.*

COTTONMOUTH
(*Calling across the clearing from his porch*)
Hey, that's a nice purty tune, One-Note.

A bearded ex-jockey, LOSER, *comes out on the porch, with* SLOW-BOY. LOSER *is still wearing the ragged remains of his racing silks.*

COTTONMOUTH
Loser, fetch me a jug o' shine. I wanna test that new batch.

LOSER *and* SLOW-BOY *head for the homemade still, adjacent to* COTTONMOUTH'S *shack, and fill up two jugs. They bring them over to the group, now joined by* COTTONMOUTH, *who takes the first swig. The explosive homemade joyjuice makes even this primitive monument shudder.*

COTTONMOUTH
Bush-lightnin'.

Meanwhile the jug is passing from LOSER *to* SAWDUST *to* BIGAMY *to* WRITER . . . *each with violent effect.*

COTTONMOUTH
(*Taking out his snake*)
Hey, Curley Cue, don' wanna leave you outa this party—but first I better milk them ever-lovin' fangs of yourn. (*He grabs* LOSER'S *jockey crop and places it between the snake's jaws. His other huge hand holds the snake's head as the venom drips out*) Now ya c'n have a drink of snake medicine jest like the rest o' these folks. Oney I trust ya more'n I do any o' these varmints. (*He opens the snake's mouth and pours a slug down its milky white throat*) He's my brother—oney difference he's too lazy t'git up 'n walk. (*As* ONE-NOTE *continues singing and playing the guitar,* COTTONMOUTH *dances off with the writhing*

snake) Look at 'im keepin' time t' the music. Ol' Curley Cue c'n dance when he's full o' bush-lightnin'.

A few yards away SLOW-BOY *is carrying the jug from one to another of the plumers.*

SLOW-BOY

Y'know, when I got up this mornin', jes' afore the sun, I waded out t' catch me some snapper fer breakfast 'n guess who was standin' there?

SAWDUST

Napoleon?

WRITER

George Washington?

BIGAMY BOB

Jim Jeffries?

SLOW-BOY
(*Seriously*)
Naw—God. Yeah, 'n he talked t'me too.

WRITER

Hey, we got ourselves a regular Joan of Arc. Sees visions 'n everything. Gonna wash away our sins, Slow-Boy?

LOSER

Ain't enough water fer that in the whole flappin' Gulf o' Mexico.

SLOW-BOY
(*Continuing, impervious*)
He's a real nice fella, God is, real nice fella. He sez to me, "How's the fishin', kid? Need any help?" He's a real nice fella.

SAWDUST
(*He cracks his long circus whip and curls it expertly around the jug* SLOW-BOY *is carrying*)
Come back with that joyjuice. You saw God!!

In the background, COTTONMOUTH *is dancing with his snake as* ONE-NOTE *continues to play and sing.*

SAWDUST

What was he wearin'?

SLOW-BOY

Well— He was barefoot and He had on some ol' pants 'n a big black hat—jest like m'daddy.

WRITER

Ha—ha—he thinks God goes around barefoot wearin' a big black hat!

All the others laugh loudly at SLOW-BOY, *to his discomfiture. Suddenly* COTTONMOUTH *strides over and knocks* SAWDUST *over with the back of his powerful hand. The music stops abruptly.*

COTTONMOUTH

Lay off. If he says him 'n God is fishin' buddies, him 'n God is fishin' buddies.

One by one the ragged little army nod and mutter obediently. For here in the lower Glades, COTTONMOUTH'S *slightest whim is a law no one dares challenge. There is an uneasy silence. Then—*

COTTONMOUTH

G'wan, One-Note, keep pickin' on that git-box.

As ONE-NOTE *strikes up a lively reel,* SAWDUST *bows to* LOSER *with mock formality.*

SAWDUST

Miss Matilda, will you do me the honor of joinin' me in the next quadrille?

LOSER

(*Coyly, in a falsetto*)

Why, thank you, Mr. Sawdust.

SAWDUST *grabs* LOSER *with comic lustiness.*

LOSER

Naughty, naughty—

In a moment the boys have jumped down from the catwalk and are dancing in the mud to the rhythms of ONE-NOTE's *gittar. Off on the side* COTTONMOUTH *senses something inaudible in the mangrove channel leading out to the river.*

COTTONMOUTH

Who's out there! Quiet! Quiet! Hey, I hear you. State your business.

GRAVEL VOICE

(*From behind mangrove*)

Fella up the way says yer friendly to bo's on the lam.

COTTONMOUTH *peers forward and sees a bestial-looking, truck-bodied, ox-jawed man of some 250 pounds, accompanied by a wiry, bonier, younger side-kick. Both are unshaved, haggard and torn.* COTTONMOUTH *and the others, who have gathered around, watch suspiciously.*

COTTONMOUTH

Who are you?

BEEF

You mean yuh didn't hear nothin' o' the bust-out at the State Pen? We was the fellas broke it open.

COTTONMOUTH

Ya got names?

BEEF

Me, Beef Minotti. (*Points to his side-kick*) Windy McGhee.

COTTONMOUTH

How do I know ya ain't marshals?

BEEF's *prolonged laugh becomes a hoarse, wheezy cough.*

BEEF

Do we look like the law? We stole a boat at Fort Myers 'n kept movin' south till we come to this—(*Looks around*)—this backside of creation.

COTTONMOUTH

(*To* WINDY)

Why don't ya say something?

BEEF

Ya mean Windy? He's deef 'n dumb. Nice fella t' lock with. Let's ya do all the talkin'.

COTTONMOUTH

What brung ya here? How'd ya come t' find it?

BEEF

An Indian showed us. Sez yer his boss. Fella with one arm called Billy.

COTTONMOUTH

Billy One-Arm. Pretty good hunter when he ain't full o' shine. Come on in. (BEEF *and* WINDY *move forward into the clearing, surrounded by the gang.* COTTONMOUTH *quickly disarms them. Then he steps up onto the porch of his shack and seats himself in his huge chair*) Think ya could survive with this crowd?

BEEF

Willin' t' try.

COTTONMOUTH

We'll see. I got a real Sunday school class here. Boys, tell 'em about yerselves.

BIGAMY BOB

They call me Bigamy Bob—did a little time fer gettin' caught with seven wives.

COTTONMOUTH

His ol' man was a preacher—told him never t' bundle with a gal unless he marry up with her.

BIGAMY BOB

Kinda got to be a habit, I guess.

COTTONMOUTH

I seen worse habits, hey, fellas? Loser!

LOSER

I useta be a jockey till they ruled me off for rough-ridin'. I could switch the whip three times from the head of the stretch to the wire.

BEEF

Mr. Also-Ran!

LOSER

Listen— I wasn't too bad, Beefhead, I won my share of the big ones, too.

COTTONMOUTH

This bum we call the Writer.

WRITER

I wrote a book in the pen—put it down word for word jest like I seen it and heard it, 'n it was so raw the warden had it taken out 'n burned with the rest of the garbage.

COTTONMOUTH

Ever he writes about us, we'll chop 'im up fer panther bait. Sawdust here useta handle lions 'n tigers in the circus.

SAWDUST

(*Touching a long scar on top of his bald head*)
Including the lion tamer's wife.

COTTONMOUTH

(*Looking over at* ONE-NOTE)
That git-fiddle player there useta work the towns with a pair of black glasses and a tin cup.

BEEF

Seems like an all-right bunch of fellas.

COTTONMOUTH

Not a single one of 'em you cain't trust—long as yuh don't turn yer back on 'em.

BEEF

How about a place to bunk?

COTTONMOUTH

Pick any shack ya want. Fight fer it 'n if ya win, it's yours. This one's mine. Ya want it?

BEEF

(Backing off and looking away)

How about that one?

The plume hunters follow BEEF *and* WINDY *apprehensively as they appraise the shacks from the catwalk.* COTTONMOUTH *and* SLOW-BOY *watch from below.*

COTTONMOUTH

(Dismissing the first shack)

They ain't here. If ya want it ya gotta wait till they git back t' fight 'em. That's the rule.

BEEF *and* WINDY *pause at the next shack. The owner,* BIGAMY, *sidles up.*

BIGAMY

My floor boards are all rotted out. Honest, yuh c'n look.

COTTONMOUTH

Shet up. Let 'em make up their own minds.

BEEF *pauses at the next,* WRITER'S.

WRITER

I didn't build any steps up to mine. Only them old boards. With your weight, it—

COTTONMOUTH

Listen! Shet up!

BEEF

Who wants it! (*The next shack really attracts* BEEF) Who belongs to this one?

LOSER

You don't want this one—the roof's leakin' somethin' awful—

SAWDUST

Yeah and the poles is fixin' t'cave in.

COTTONMOUTH

When I say shet up—!!!

> BEEF *points to the shack belonging to* LOSER *and* SAW-DUST, *indicating it is his choice. Everyone looks at* LOSER *and* SAWDUST, *then at the formidable* BEEF *and his lean, silent side-kick. The atmosphere becomes tense and silent.*

SAWDUST

(*Whispering to his diminutive partner*)

Loser, you take the big one.

LOSER

Me?

SAWDUST

(*Persuasively*)

That way I c'n take out the smaller fella quick while you're duckin' around. Then the two of us can handle the big hippo together. Okay?

LOSER

Okay.

> *The issue is joined. The contestants jump down from the ramp into the "ring," sinking at least a half foot into the mud.* SAWDUST *choses* WINDY *and moves in on him confidently. To everyone's amazement,* WINDY *turns out*

to be a lightning-fast, spectacular fighter. Before the slower, clumsy SAWDUST *knows what hit him,* WINDY *has cleverly feinted him, and struck him half a dozen telling blows in succession, almost knocking him down.*

WRITER

You couldn't tame a sick tiger cub, Sawdust.

The crowd laughs at SAWDUST'S *discomfiture.* WINDY *moves in for the kill—one, two, one-two, the last a snaky right to the jaw, and* SAWDUST *is not only down but out cold—in the mud.*

COTTONMOUTH
(Matter of factly)

Drag that bum outa the way.

Now LOSER, *left to his own resources, pulls off his filthy sweater and stands in his tattered jockey outfit, crop in hand, ready for the fight.* BEEF *waits impassively.*

SLOW-BOY *has brought* COTTONMOUTH'S *chair and this monarch of the mangrove sits comfortably, ready to enjoy himself,* CURLEY CUE *in hand.*

LOSER *sweats as he realizes he must face* BEEF *alone.*

WRITER

Go easy on him, Loser.

COTTONMOUTH

If yuh wanna quit now, yuh c'n save yerself a lickin'.

LOSER

Let's go. Worst he c'n do is kill me. I won't promise not to use my knees 'n teeth 'n everything else I got.

WRITER

Loser's got to hit him below the belt—he can't reach no higher.

BIGAMY

I'll lay yuh five feathers to a single Loser goes down with the first lick.

COTTONMOUTH

Bet! Five more he draws first blood.

Meanwhile, LOSER *is circling cautiously around* BEEF— *a flyweight against an oversized heavyweight whose fists look as big as* LOSER's *head.*

BIGAMY

Put a saddle on him, Loser.

Everyone laughs. Then suddenly the action starts. As BEEF *lunges in, the quick-footed ex-jockey ducks under his heavy arms and knees him. As* BEEF *bellows his pain and bends over,* LOSER's *tough little head smashes up against the bigger man's nose. It gushes blood. The squatters roar with delight.*

COTTONMOUTH

First blood—my five!

BEEF *literally has his blood up now. He is more wary. He crouches and his huge forearms form more of a barrier. He lunges at* LOSER, *who manages to avoid several haymakers, and then* LOSER *jumps on* BEEF's *back and begins to beat him with his crop.*

WRITER

Attaway, Loser. Kick 'im, bite 'im, scratch 'im, dig your spurs into 'im!

BEEF *finally manages to unseat his tormentor and lands a punch that connects.* LOSER *reels backwards.* BEEF *lumbers after him.*

ONE-NOTE

Give up, Loser.

COTTONMOUTH

Give up, hell!

> LOSER *sinks his teeth into the fat muscle of* BEEF's *arm.* BEEF *howls, lashes at his midget antagonist and a terrible blow practically lifts* LOSER *off the ground and topples him, apparently unconscious, into the mud.*

COTTONMOUTH

I'll take ten to one Loser gets up!

WRITER

You got it!

COTTONMOUTH

(*Rises from his chair and stands over the fallen* LOSER)
Git up, Loser.

WRITER

Git up? He's dead.

COTTONMOUTH

I said: Git up! Git up, I'm bettin' on yuh— SO, GIT UP! (LOSER *faintly hears the command. His bloody head is buried in mud. Painfully he tries to lift himself and slowly succeeds in rising to one knee*) Try harder! HARDER! (LOSER *make a supreme effort. On rubbery legs, his face a bloody mask, he manages to rise. Feebly he tries to brace himself and lift his hands against* BEEF's *coup de grace*) When ah tells 'em t' git up, they *git up.*

> BEEF *picks up the barely conscious* LOSER *and smashes him down for the last time into the mud. Then* BEEF *and* WINDY *go off to claim their shack.* WRITER *walks over to the still stretched-out* SAWDUST.

WRITER

Mornin', Sawdust, have a nice nap?

COTTONMOUTH
(*Picks up* LOSER *and carries him into his shack*)
Loser, yuh c'n bunk with me 'n the kid.

FADE OUT

FADE IN: MIAMI RIVER—SUNSET

As WALT'S *boat approaches* MORGAN'S *yacht, tied up at the dock. The canvas canoe is now considerably changed in appearance. It is mud-stained and saw grass has slashed the canvas.* WALT, *too, has undergone a change. His shirt is open, his khaki trousers are no longer tucked neatly into his boots—in fact, he has discarded his boots: signs of learning to live with the Glades.*

Behind MORGAN'S *sailing vessel are old houses, the graceful coconut palms, tropical flowering plants. A colorful fishing boat of the period glides by. Farther down the dock fishermen are drying their nets. The scene suggests the enchantment of tropical Florida as twilight spreads its roseate pastels along the waterfront.*

In the stern, being served coconut drinks by MORGAN, *are* NATHANSON *and* NAOMI, *who is fetchingly dressed in a semiformal orange gown of the period. From the road along the dock comes the sound of an automobile horn honking furiously. A brand-new Cadillac driven by* GEORGE LIGGETT, *with* MRS. LIGGETT *clinging to his arm, races into view. A horse-drawn carriage, children, dogs, etc., scramble out of the path of destruction.*

MRS. LIGGETT
George, slow down.

HORSE CARRIAGE OCCUPANT
(*Angrily*)
Look where you're going, you speed demon!

LIGGETT

(*Pulling on the brake*)

Stop cluttering up the road with those old-fashioned buggies. (*Looks over and sees* NATHANSON) Hello there, Aaron, how do you like my new machine? One of these days you ought to get yourself a Cadillac.

NATHANSON

(*Amiably looking at* LIGGETT's *Cadillac*)

I hope you break your fool neck in it, George.

> *Suddenly, as if out of control, the car lunges forward with a great roar.* MRS. LIGGETT *holds onto her motoring hat and screams.*

NATHANSON

(*Holding up his drink as the sound of the car diminishes*)

Well, here's to Miami in spite of George Liggett.

> WALT, *barefoot, has climbed aboard on the other side of the yacht, and come upon them suddenly. His face is streaked with dirt, his hair is askew, his mood is one of exhilaration.*

WALT

I'll drink to that.

NAOMI

(*Crossing to him*)

Well—you're a mess.

MORGAN

Welcome, back, lad.

NATHANSON

In two days you look changed—almost wild.

WALT

I'm afraid I jettisoned half the stuff I bought. They are now markers from your store for thirty miles between here and Chikikee Hammock.

> NAOMI *hurries to the cabin.*

MORGAN

Then you got there?

WALT

Yes, I got there.

MORGAN

Good boy. And you posted the rookery.

NAOMI *returns with a towel.*

NAOMI

What a pair. So full of questions you haven't even asked him to sit down—(*Wiping his face*) For the scratches on your face. And—(*Handing him a coconut*) Ross Morgan's latest invention, brandy and coconut milk.

MORGAN

I call it the Miami Surprise. Aaron, are you ready for another one?

NATHANSON

Ross, at my age one surprise a day is enough.

MORGAN

Naomi?

NAOMI

I'm game.

NATHANSON

Game? Did you ever hear such language? Naomi and her American slang. Since when does a well-brought-up young lady accept a second drink?

NAOMI

Poppa, you tried very hard, but I'm not a well-brought-up young lady. I'm me.

NATHANSON

(*Shaking his head good-naturedly*)

There's a saying in the old country—better to rear a serpent in the nest than an independent daughter.

NAOMI
You shouldn't mention serpents to a man who's been out there with snakes and alligators. I'm sure he'd like to forget everything about the Glades for a little while.

WALT
(*Persuasively*)
I don't see how anybody who goes deep into that country can ever forget it—(MORGAN *smiles, knowingly*)—the strangeness of it—the bigness of it—it's—well, it's as if a river was a prairie fifty miles across—or the prairie was a river—the grass and the water run together, and there are islands—these hammocks—thousands of them—as far as the eye can see—just grass and water and islands and clouds, the fattest whitest clouds in the biggest bluest sky I ever saw—and the life—it's all around you —under the water, in the shallows, in the trees, winging over-head—the birds—egrets and herons as white as the clouds—blue herons that melt into the sky—and roseate spoonbills the color of twilight—(*Pauses; his listeners seem spellbound*)—the colors, the sounds, the size, the wild orchids, the water lilies—(*He breaks off, embarrassed*) You've got to see it for yourself.

MORGAN
Now you see what I mean.

NATHANSON
Young man, you're right—there's no wilderness like it in the whole world—three million acres of unexplored frontier—only I'd like to see it used as—

NAOMI
(*Lightly, handing* WALT *a second coconut drink*)
If Walt has to hear that drainage speech, he deserves another drink.

NATHANSON

It's not a speech. I'm not a politician like George Liggett trying to sell underwater land at so much a quart. I see a whole network of canals crisscrossing the Glades, bringing the wasteland
into cultivation.

MORGAN

A noble dream—for you, Aaron.

NATHANSON

(*Rising, excited*)

Look around you—isn't Miami a noble dream? America is
full of noble dreams springing into reality. If little Holland
could say to the mighty ocean, under your shallows you have
land a-plenty that you don't need and we can take back and turn
into a garden spot, if little Holland could do that, what about
us?

WALT

Sure it could be done. But there's something to be said for
leaving it just as it is—the only Everglades in the whole world.

NATHANSON

(*Taking out a large colored map*)

Look, I happen to have this map with me.

NAOMI

Happen to! Poppa, you know you sleep with that map.

NATHANSON

(*Spreading map out*)

If I can only sell my idea to the Improvement Commission before the speculators gobble up that land. Liggett has been pay-
ing a dollar an acre and selling for ten—selling suckers on the
idea the State will do the draining. I know they won't unless we
come up with a sound plan, a thorough survey, and son, you're
just who I've been looking for to head it up.

WALT

Mr. Nathanson, beyond this river lies an unexplored empire all right, and now that I've seen it I want to help keep it an empire, a sanctuary for wild life.—

NATHANSON

What chance have you against the land pirates in Miami and the feather pirates in the Glades? You and I could be partners in the progress of South Florida.

WALT

(*With deep, quiet conviction*)

Sir, progress and I never got along very well. Maybe that's what draws me into the Glades. You see—they're—well, they're sort of the way the world must have looked on the first day, when it was all water, full of prehistoric life, and then the first land beginning to rise out of the sea . . . it was all there before man—you feel the life force in there in its purest, earliest form —and then Cain and the brothers of Cain raise their twelve-gauge shotguns and fire into the face of God.

They all look at each other in silence a moment. Then MORGAN's *rising breaks the mood.*

MORGAN

You see, Aaron, now that we've finally got ourselves a warden —don't go trying to steal him out from under my nose. (*Leading* NATHANSON *forward*)— I've been wanting to show you the wireless telephone I've just installed—I think it may be the first one in Florida.

MORGAN *and* NATHANSON *move forward, into the cabin, out of view.* NAOMI *joins* WALT, *who leans on the boom around which the sail is furled.*

NAOMI

I knew it was more than just saving those birds. The way you talked about it I feel—some mystery in there caught hold of you.

WALT

I wish you could have seen this fellow Cottonmouth, the fellow they call the King of the Glades. He's filthy, he slaughters those birds like a butcher, they even say he's a murderer—and yet—there's something about him, something that's, well, free in a primeval way that most of us have lost the knack of knowing how to be.

NAOMI

Ross calls him a brute, a menace to society. You almost sound as if you admire him.

WALT

He is a brute—but there's a kind of defiance, some basic truth in him that appeals to me—a sort of fierce poetry about the way he moves through the Glades, as ugly and as beautiful as the cottonmouths he handles like kittens.

NAOMI

Ugly, beautiful and deadly.

WALT

It—it may sound crazy, but even while I'm scheming how to take him, I'm looking forward to seeing him again.

NAOMI

Worse than crazy, it's a disease. Here on the river they call it Glades fever. Nobody knows how many men have followed that river into the Glades and never come out.

WALT

It's not as hopeless as all that. If you know how to blaze a trail, live off the land, keep your wits about you . . .

NAOMI

Last year a man raised in Everglades went hunting in Lostman's River. Someone stole his boat and in one single night he was eaten to death by mosquitoes.

WALT

A mosquito bar and some kerosene might do the trick.

NAOMI

Why do you think they call it Lostman's River?

WALT

Lostman's River. Shark River. There's something about the sound of them. Great unknown rivers teeming with fish, alive with birds, Lostman's River. I hope I can find it.

NAOMI

(*A little bitterly*)

Oh, you'll find it. You'll find your friend Cottonmouth. You'll find everything you're looking for.

Her eyes challenge him. He makes a move toward her. She turns away.

DISSOLVE

COTTONMOUTH KEY—TWILIGHT

COTTONMOUTH overlooks the activities from the porch of his large shack. In the clearing the squatters are roasting wild suckling pigs on spits over a large open fire.

Behind the barbecue SAWDUST *and* BEEF *are teasing* SLOW-BOY. COTTONMOUTH *spies them. He picks up a knife and throws it. The knife lands in a roast pig, inches from* SAWDUST's *hand, and quivers there.* SAWDUST *and* BEEF *look shamefacedly in the direction of* COTTONMOUTH. COTTONMOUTH *is satisfied he has been obeyed.*

PERFESSER *and* THUMBS *appear, and approach* COTTONMOUTH's *porch.*

COTTONMOUTH

Well, Perfesser, where ya been?

PERFESSER

If I may elucidate—uh—

COTTONMOUTH

Perfesser! (PERFESSER *hands over the money paid by* LIGGETT *for the egret plumes in Miami*) What's the news?

PERFESSER

I took the liberty of checking up on our new bird-boy. He's no panty-waist. Holds his likker and smokes big black cigars and he's pretty handy with his dukes. We had an opportunity to observe him immediately upon his arrival.

SAWDUST *enters during this speech and hands* COTTON-MOUTH *his knife.*

COTTONMOUTH

I've seen him. What's the news?

PERFESSER

He's comin' back in.

COTTONMOUTH

What I figgered.

SAWDUST

Any guy who's crazy enough to worry about savin' birds is crazy enough to make trouble.

COTTONMOUTH

He'll die o' natural causes. Ain't a better way to git shut of a foreigner. (*Pauses*) Okay, I made up my mind. Sawdust, you take Billy 'n pole into Miamuh.

SAWDUST *rouses the sleeping* BILLY, *who is lying at the end of* COTTONMOUTH'S *porch, dressed in the colorful shirt of the Seminoles.*

COTTONMOUTH *hands the snake he is playing with to* SLOW-BOY.

COTTONMOUTH

Kid, take Curley Cue 'n find him a nice fat frog fer his supper. Hey, One-Note, play me a nice sad song 'bout kissin' 'n killin'.

COTTONMOUTH *rocks contentedly as* ONE-NOTE *raises his plaintive, cracker voice in song.*

DISSOLVE

INTERIOR MRS. BRADFORD'S—NORTH MIAMI—NIGHT

This is rather a posh establishment for early Miami, decorated in only slightly overdone Victorian elegance. There is an ornate mahogany bar, small tables, Victorian couches, reproductions of some typical bad painting of the period, and room for dancing, with piano music provided by a young, stylish Negro who bangs out ragtime and nascent jazz somewhat in the manner of Jelly Roll Morton. In the smoky back room we can see the green tables of various games, with a number of men gambling, some attended by MRS. BRADFORD'S *attractive hostesses. A red-carpeted curving stairway leads to the second floor, where private gambling rooms are indicated. At the bar three or four girls are drinking with prospective players. One of these is* GEORGE LIGGETT, *accompanied by his English flunkey, and flanked by two hostesses, a pert young blonde and a spirited Southern brunette.* WALT *is just entering and making his way to the bar.*

LIGGETT

(*Glancing toward* WALT)

How did he get in here? Set them up for everybody, Louis, except that fellow at the end. He's a trouble-maker. I'm feeling lucky tonight.

WALT *puts his own money on the bar as* LOUIS *pours champagne for* LIGGETT'S *party.*

YOUNG BRUNETTE

Mr. Liggett, you're a darlin'.

LIGGETT

How old are you, Miss Lucy?

MISS LUCY

Goin' on twenty-one.

LIGGETT
(*To the little blonde*)

And you, my dear.

YOUNG GIRL

I'm just nineteen.

LIGGETT

Nineteen and twenty-one. Those'll be the first numbers I play. And if they pay off, you get half my winnings.

MISS LUCY
(*Taking his arm*)

Mr. Liggett, you are simply ado'rable.

LIGGETT

Shall we go, ladies.

LIGGETT, *with a girl on either arm, heads toward the rooms upstairs. As he does so, he passes* MRS. BRADFORD *playing chess with* JUDGE TIPPINS.

MRS. BRADFORD
(*Looking up at the girls approvingly*)

There's nothing like a pretty girl to change a careful bettor into a reckless plunger. (*She moves a chess piece seemingly without even studying the board, and keeps up a rapid chatter*) Oh, Judge, ah jes' can hardly wait fohr you t' make the nex' move—oh, ah've got you in such a trap ah'm so proud o' myself —ah jes' can't hardly stand it—ah realize ladies aren't supposed t' have the brain powah for a deep-thinkin' game like chess, but evah since you taught me how to move all those darlin' little pieces ah'm jest—

52

Throughout the above, JUDGE TIPPINS *is trying to make a move, then losing his concentration in the stream of* MRS. BRADFORD'S *constant chatterboxing.*

JUDGE TIPPINS

Mrs. Bradford, you are the only person I know who plays chess as if it were a ladies sewing and gossip circle. After all, chess was meant to be a quiet, contemplative game.

MRS. BRADFORD

Oh, ah know you keep tellin' me that. But ah jest cain't help it, I get so excited, especially when I move those little horses— (*As she chatters she jumps her knight over several of the* JUDGE'S *key pieces, to his chagrin*) The way they go hippity-hop, jump- ity-jump, it reminds me of mah fox-huntin' days in the Blue Ridge country before dear poor Mr. Bradford passed away—he didn't exactly pass away—he just gave up and moved west. (*She looks at the board, where she now has the* JUDGE'S *king sur- rounded*) Why ah do declare, ah have you in checkmate and didn't even realize it.

The JUDGE, *resigned to* MRS. BRADFORD'S *ways, calls over to the bar.*

JUDGE

Another bourbon, Louis. Better make that a double.

PRETTY GIRL

Oh, let me get it for you, your honor.

MRS. BRADFORD

(*Rising and calling sharply to one of her dancing hostesses, who is entwined with* LIGGETT'S *Englishman*)

Why, Miss Denise!! (*Going up to her*) Shame, shame, *shame* on you. Much, much too close. You know I insist on six inches between the dancers.

MISS DENISE
(*Broadly*)

Ain't it awful, Mabel?

MRS. BRADFORD

That will do. You may go to your room. I will not tolerate any vulgar displays on the main floor of my establishment. I'm not a prude but there's a time and place for everything.

ENGLISHMAN

Quite.

MISS DENISE *hurries off with a rear-view flounce.* MRS. BRADFORD *sees* WALT *at the bar and goes over to him.*

MRS. BRADFORD

Good evenin'. Ah'm Mrs. Bradford. Ah do believe ah saw you at the depot. Ah think it's simply noble of you to try to protect those poor defenseless birds.

WALT
(*Lightly*)

Mrs. Bradford, it seems to me when I last saw you, you were wearing several of those poor defenseless birds.

MRS. BRADFORD

Oh—now let me see. I must pick out someone very special for such a refined young gentleman—there's Gloria Stowe—you know she's related to the Stowes of Savannah.

We can see that MISS GLORIA STOWE, *coming down the stairs, may affect the part but doesn't quite make it as the flower of Southern society.*

SAWDUST
(*Who has been watching* WALT *from the porthole behind the bar that leads outside to the Rough Bar*)

Stowes of Savannah. I know her old man Six-Finger Harry, the finest pickpocket between here and Jacksonville.

WALT

(*To* MRS. BRADFORD)

Thank you, ma'am, but I think I'll just stand at the bar and have a whiskey.

MRS. BRADFORD

(*Taking her leave*)

Have fun.

SAWDUST

Louis, break out the best bourbon in the house for my young friend.

WALT

Thank you, but I don't think we've been—

SAWDUST

We're all one big happy family here in Miami. Say, aren't you the fella was up into the Glades the other day lookin' around?

WALT

(*Picking up the glass* SAWDUST *has filled*)

Uh-huh. Guess everybody knows about it by now. Even that gang out there on Cottonmouth Key.

SAWDUST

Well, more power to you, if you're really goin' in after 'em.

WALT

Thank you, sir.

SAWDUST *has now disappeared behind the porthole.*

EXTERIOR ROUGH BAR

A group of disreputable-looking men are standing around. BILLY ONE-ARM *can be seen near* SAWDUST, *who takes out a toupee and puts it on his head lovingly. Using a whiskey bottle for a mirror, he adjusts the toupee and turns toward—*

INTERIOR MRS. BRADFORD'S

SAWDUST *enters to the bar and finds a place next to* WALT.

55

SAWDUST

Hey—it's me. I always put this on when I come in—the girls seem to like it better. Here—have a drink. (*He pours another for* WALT) Son, I've gone pretty deep into those Glades, selling sewing machines to Seminoles—that's one paleface gadget them Injuns is crazy about. Your first day is nothing compared with polin' five, six days through saw grass and swamp water and mud and hammocks infested with snakes and panthers and Jersey hummingbirds, as we call the skeeters. And not a landmark a stranger can recognize between here and the hundred man-killin' miles to Cottonmouth Key.

WALT

(*Finishing off his drink*)

I'm buying this time.

SAWDUST

Hear me good, boy. You try goin' in there on your own you're gonna wind up 'gator bait.

WALT

As a matter of fact I've been looking for a guide.

SAWDUST

Then I think I got the man for you. He's a Seminole name of Billy One-Arm. Nobody every moved through that country like the Seminoles. You can be stuck in mud and marl up to your waist and a Seminole will know the secret canals, shortcuts and escape channels no white man would ever dream were there. That's why we could never lick 'em. Billy One-Arm—there's your man.

WALT

I was told Seminoles would guide you out of the Glades but never in.

SAWDUST

This one's different. Took a hunter into the Glades once for a gallon of shine. The Council voted to throw him out of the tribe. Now he works as a guide. You won't find a better one between here and Cape Sable.

WALT

What makes you so interested in helping me?

SAWDUST

Son, I've been in and out of those swamps too many times to want to see a nice young fella like you tangle with 'em single-handed. It takes two—remember that—it aways takes two.

WALT

(*Just a little drunk now*)

A Seminole who can find the old waterways. That could be a big help.

SAWDUST

Drink'er down, son, 'n we'll ankle around to the Rough Bar. That's where Billy One-Arm hangs out. Miz Bradford is kinda particular who she exposes her sweet, refined young ladies to.

As WALT *leaves with* SAWDUST, MRS. BRADFORD *is back at the chess table with her* JUDGE. *The music plays on.*

DISSOLVE

INTERIOR HALLWAY OF NATHANSON LIVING QUARTERS—NIGHT

WALT, *somewhat disheveled, slightly staggering, fumbles at what he thinks is his own door.*

NAOMI'S VOICE

(*From behind door*)

Who is it—Sam Tigertail?

WALT

(*With a little whiskey-happy laugh*)

No—it's Walt Birdwing.

NAOMI *opens the door and steps out into the hallway in her kimono.*

57

WALT

Been up to North Miami. Got myself an Indian guide to go back into the Glades with me tomorrow. I'm all set.

NAOMI

You look it. You need a guide to find your own room.

WALT

Now, now, let's not quarrel—just when I'm ready to go—

NAOMI

(*Leading him down hall to his door*)

To *bed*—that's where you're ready to go.

WALT

I've been up at Mrs. Bradford's and there were one—two—three murders, just like you said. Only I wasn't one of 'em, 'least I don't think so. I got back, didn't I?

NAOMI

Barely. Here, this is your room. (*Opening door*) Maybe I'd better help you.

INTERIOR WALT'S BEDROOM

As NAOMI *pilots him in.*

WALT

You're wunnerful, Naomi, you know that? Even if you do smoke cigarettes. You're the most—the most—

NAOMI

Tell me about it in the morning.

WALT

(*Sitting on his bed*)

Be gone in the morning. With this Seminole. Wunnerful fellow. Real professional guide. Knows lotsa secret canals. Says he can take me all the way to Lostman's River.

NAOMI

Floating in a bottle, I suppose.

WALT

(*With whiskied seriousness*)

No, sir, in a real Seminole dugout. With Billy One-Arm, they call 'im 'cause when he was a kid a 'gator chewed off the other one.

NAOMI

(*Helping him off with his shoes*)

I wouldn't trust anybody I met in North Miami.

WALT

Billy's a Seminole. And Seminoles never lie. You know that, Naomi. Billy's my friend.

NAOMI

Uh-huh. Did you find enough girls?

WALT

Girls? Oh yeah, Mrs. Bradford introduced me to a charming young lady—Miss er-Miss—but anyway she comes from one of the best families in Savannah—

NAOMI

All of Mrs. Bradford's protégées come from the best families in Savannah—

WALT

Now—now let's not fight. Anyway when I saw all those girls, all those lovely creatures of refinement and culture—I didn't even feel like dancing with 'em, Naomi, that's a fact. I just kept wishing one of 'em would turn out to be you.

NAOMI

(*Rather touched, but kidding him*)

Oh! So now you're trying to put me to work at Mrs. Bradford's.

WALT

No—that's not what I mean. What I was trying to say was—well, it's—you know what I mean.

NAOMI

What time are you meeting that "wunnerful Indian" of yours?

WALT

Promised Billy meet 'im at the dock sunup. Never lie t' a Seminole.

NAOMI

Yes, I know. You'd better get some rest now.
> *She turns out the small reading light over his head.*

WALT

Aren't you going to kiss me good night? A little reward for resisting Mrs. Bradford's little flowers?

NAOMI

You've gotten awfully fresh since your trip to North Miami.
> WALT *lies back on the bed, illuminated only by the moonlight filtering through the window. Suddenly* NAOMI *is kneeling over him, kissing him firmly on the mouth.*

WALT
(Whispering)
What made you change your mind?

NAOMI

Suddenly I felt like it. Remember, I'm *me*.

WALT

Naomi . . .
> *He reaches out to draw her closer, but she rises and goes.*

NAOMI
(At the door)
Good night. Sleep well.

Intrigued, a little baffled, WALT *watches the door close behind her.*

DISSOLVE

EVERGLADES—EARLY MORNING

WALT *in his canoe follows* BILLY ONE-ARM *in his long, narrow cypress dugout along a ten-foot wide canal, the seemingly endless expanse of prairie behind them.* BILLY *turns off into a still narrower canal.*

The sun is beating down strongly. BILLY *is purposely setting a tiring pace.* WALT *is sweating. He slaps at mosquitoes on his face.*

DISSOLVE

EVERGLADES SHOAL

The water is only a few inches deep here, covered by hyacinths. In the background is a swamp filled with cypress trees. BILLY *and* WALT *are barely able to move their boats.*

WALT

This doesn't look like a secret canal to me.

BILLY

Canal gone. Weeds grow too fast.

DISSOLVE

EVERGLADES PRAIRIE—DAY

WALT *and* BILLY *are paddling in water a foot deep, but it has suddenly begun to rain, a brief slashing tropical downpour, soaking them.*

DISSOLVE

EVERGLADES—DEEP MUD—LATE AFTERNOON

The marl is waist deep. Progress is tortuous. WALT *is becoming exhausted.*

DISSOLVE

EVERGLADES—TWILIGHT

> *Now they are on moving water at last.* BILLY *is quite far ahead.* WALT's *face is bloody from swatted mosquitoes, saw grass and low branches. They approach a hammock and land.*

DISSOLVE

HAMMOCK CAMP SITE—NIGHT

> WALT *is restlessly trying to get to sleep in a bed-roll under his mosquito bar. Nearby,* BILLY ONE-ARM *is already sound asleep. The night sounds of the Glades are insistent —the telltale cough of the alligators, the myriad-throated chorus of frogs, the haunting owls, the eerie cry of the limpkins, night herons and other sleepless birds. An infernal racket. Outside the mosquito bar a smoke-fire is burning, to keep the insects away. But they collect on the netting, a forbidding assortment.* WALT's *rest is disturbed by the various night prowlers of this jungle—a black bear, a panther, a wildcat, raccoons climbing, owls, alligators moving out of their crawls.*
>
> WALT *hears a mysterious scratching outside the netting, and discovers a burrowing crab, like some monster in a horror film, with its hideous eyes on antenna-like stems, its stilt-like legs and ability to send forth jets of inky liquid. Seemingly oblivious to all this,* BILLY ONE-ARM *is apparently still fast asleep alongside the fire. But when* WALT *rolls over and finally begins to doze,* BILLY *rises stealthily and hurriedly tiptoes away from the camp.* WALT *senses the defection, rouses himself, lifts the flap of the mosquito bar and starts running through the mangrove.*

WALT

(Shouting)

Billy!

Hurrying toward his dugout, BILLY *hears* WALT's *cries and stops for a moment, knife in hand. As* WALT *runs in,* BILLY *turns around, shamefacedly. His days in the Glades with* WALT—*the white man's easy camaraderie and his determination under pressure have been undermining* BILLY's *willingness to abandon* WALT *to his fate.*

WALT

Billy! Why did you run away from me?

BILLY

(*Evasively*)

Billy go catch frogs. I cook for you.

WALT

Don't lie to me, Billy. I thought you Seminoles never lied.

BILLY

Billy lie to his tribe once. Tribe say, "Go live with white man."

WALT

I know about your people, Billy . . . how you were driven from good land to bad land and finally to this—no land at all.

BILLY

Enough land. We live.

WALT

You and the birds, eh, Billy? But each year fewer birds, fewer Seminoles.

BILLY

(*Intent, impressed*)

I think. You say my tribe like the birds. Some white men kill. Some white men help. (*He studies* WALT *a moment, then smiles gravely*) I never meet white man like you.

There is a moment's silence, as they both seem to realize the significance of what BILLY *is thinking. A bird calls from a tree overhead.*

63

WALT
(*Offering* BILLY *a cigar*)
I forgot to bring along my peace pipe but how about puffing on a peace cigar?

> BILLY *accepts the cigar. He grins appreciatively.* WALT *turns inland toward higher ground as he puffs his cigar. Noticing a strange tree, he moves toward it and is about to examine the leaves when* BILLY, *seeing this, hurries forward.*

BILLY
(*Crying out as he grabs* WALT's *arm*)
Don't touch! Don't touch! Bad poison!

WALT
(*Drawing back*)
Huh?

BILLY
Tree—manchineel. Burns skin like fire. Never go near! Never touch!

WALT
It's lucky I've got you with me.

BILLY
Maybe not so lucky for Billy.

> BILLY *looks at* WALT. *He is torn between his new-found friendship for this white man and his fear of* COTTONMOUTH's *retaliation.*

DISSOLVE

COTTONMOUTH KEY—COOK SHACK—MORNING
> *This is a communal open-air kitchen, raised off the ground and palmetto-roofed, on the style of a Seminole chikee.* PERFESSER *and* WRITER *are serving a stew cooked in an old-fashioned wood stove. All the members of the*

gang are present. A tense atmosphere prevails. COTTON-
MOUTH *is not in sight.*

SAWDUST

He's been quiet so long it's made me lose my appetite.
Suddenly COTTONMOUTH *appears, headed toward the
cook shack at a rapid pace.*

WRITER

Here it comes.

COTTONMOUTH

Billy shoulda been back afore sunup.

WRITER

Yeah, we figgered by high noon today Bird-Boy'd be makin' a
nice light meal for the buzzards.

COTTONMOUTH

Go find them. Bring me Billy.

WRITER

How do you want Bird-Boy? Roasted whole or in little
pieces?

COTTONMOUTH

Don't go carvin' up Bird-Boy. Just leave 'im.

PERFESSER

But, your highness, what if he defies the elements by means
of his scientific—

COTTONMOUTH

No killin' till I say so. Bring me Billy! Now get goin'!
*His men leave their meals half-eaten, jump down from
the shack and hurry off in the direction of their boats.*

DISSOLVE

EVERGLADES—DAY

WALT *and* BILLY *in their boats are coming down a wide
canal. On one of the banks a young Seminole woman is*

washing clothes, pounding them with a pestle in the manner of her people. Close by her a little girl in a colorful ankle-length skirt is tossing hyacinth blossoms into the water. As WALT *and* BILLY *approach,* BILLY *calls out a few words in Seminole. There is no response from the young woman.*

WALT

Who is she, Billy?

BILLY

She my wife and child. I come this way to see them.

WALT

You want to go ashore?

BILLY

No. Tribe say she never talk to me again.

The two men paddle past. As they disappear around the bend in the canal, the woman stops washing and looks for a long time after them.

DISSOLVE

EVERGLADES WATERWAYS—DAY

As three pairs of plume hunters approach, each boat choosing a different fork. One of them, poled by WRITER *and* SAWDUST, *turns in the direction* WALT *and* BILLY *have been moving.*

DISSOLVE

HAMMOCK CAMP SITE—WRITER AND SAWDUST —AFTERNOON

As they discover BILLY *and* WALT's *smoldering fire.*

WRITER

Looks like a Seminole fire. Could be Billy's.

SAWDUST

Looks like a nice cozy little breakfast for two.
They hurry back to their boat.

DISSOLVE

ANOTHER HAMMOCK—NIGHTFALL

WRITER *and* SAWDUST *approach, dock their boats, and climb ashore.*

SAME HAMMOCK—CAMP SITE—NIGHTFALL

WALT *and* BILLY *are seated in front of a small fire roasting frogs' legs.* BILLY *suddenly becomes alert.*

BILLY

Somebody come. I think I know who it is. I throw them off track. I come back for you. Don't call.

BILLY *darts off, toward the bank where he had tied his dugout. As* BILLY *emerges from the brush,* WRITER *and* SAWDUST *grab him, one on each side.* BILLY *cries out.*

WRITER

Yuh started yer career lying to Seminoles. Looks like yer gonna wind it up lying to Cottonmouth.

After a brief, intense struggle they drag BILLY *off.*

By the time WALT *comes running up to where he and* BILLY *had left their boats,* WRITER, SAWDUST *and* BILLY *are barely discernible, poling rapidly away.* WALT'S *boat and* BILLY'S *dugout have been slashed and hacked into uselessness. Food and equipment have been dumped into the water. Futilely he fires a few shots into the darkness. From far away comes a taunting laugh.*

SAWDUST

It's a long walk back to Miamuh, Bird-Boy. I'll kiss them Bradford gals goodby fer ya.

Bitterly WALT *peers into the dark waterway into which* BILLY ONE-ARM *has disappeared.*

DISSOLVE

COTTONMOUTH KEY

SAWDUST *and* WRITER *are poling in.* BILLY *is seated between them.*

Standing majestically on the back portico of his shack, which overlooks the canal approach to his settlement, is COTTONMOUTH. *Surrounding him are* SLOW-BOY, BEEF, LOSER, PERFESSER, BIGAMY, THUMBS, ONE-NOTE *and* WINDY, *the infernal jurors of* COTTONMOUTH'S *kangaroo court.*

PERFESSER

Where did you find him?

WRITER

In Alligator Bay.

The men look on ominously as SAWDUST *poles the skiff to a stop directly under* COTTONMOUTH.

COTTONMOUTH

(*Glaring down at* BILLY)

Yuh knowed my orders was t' lose 'im. Why didn't you lose 'im?

BILLY

Bird-Boy pretty smart.

COTTONMOUTH

Billy, yuh took up with 'im. 'Stead of losin' 'im yuh was helpin' 'im.

BILLY

In night wise owl say to Billy, "Don't hurt Bird-Boy. Bird-Boy good man."

COTTONMOUTH

Wise owl—hogwash! Yuh dare to sit there 'n tell me what to think!

BILLY

Bird-Boy make me to see Seminoles like the birds. Bird-Boy make me see white man not all the same. Some like white heron. (*He rises in the boat and looks directly at* COTTONMOUTH) Some like black turkey buzzard.

COTTONMOUTH

Heard enough. Trial's over. I find yuh guilty. All in favor?

PLUME GANG

Aye! Give it to 'im! Guilty! Stinkin' traitor! String 'im up!

SAWDUST

Hang him!

COTTONMOUTH

Hanging's too good fer 'im. Give 'im the manchineel.

BILLY

Hang Billy! Shoot Billy! No manchineel!

COTTONMOUTH

Manchineel.

BEEF

Manchineel? What kind of rap is that?

PERFESSER

Manchineel. *Hippomane Mancinella*—produces a sap that destroys the mucous membranes, causing swelling of the eyes, lips, tongue and other discomforts. The Carib Indians used it to poison their arrows. Forgive the jest if I say it is the only tree that can carve its initials on you.

BEEF *laughs obscenely.*

As SAWDUST *and* WRITER *start to pole him away,* BILLY *looks back at* COTTONMOUTH, *begging for a reprieve.*

BILLY

No manchineel! No manchineel! (COTTONMOUTH *is silent as he watches the skiff round the bend out of Lostman's River.*

BILLY's *cries of protest diminish:*) No manchineel . . . no manchineel . . .

DISSOLVE

MANGROVE SWAMP

From the distance a terrible cry of pain reaches WALT. *Changing his course, he plunges on through the knee-deep muck of the mangrove swamp.*

DISSOLVE

EVERGLADES PRAIRIE

BILLY's *wife,* SUZY-BILLY, *having heard* BILLY's *screams, is poling her small dugout across a far-flung prairie of saw grass.*

DISSOLVE

MANCHINEEL TREE—DAWN

BILLY ONE-ARM *is lashed to the manchineel tree, which has been pierced so that its deadly sap can more quickly take effect. The results are horrifying:* BILLY's *face and chest are swollen with red-purple blisters. His cries and his ordeal are over now.*

Kneeling at his feet, SUZY-BILLY *is murmuring a Seminole prayer, when* WALT *approaches. His clothes are badly torn and he shows the effects of insect bites, fatigue, and extreme exposure to the elements. He stares in horror at* BILLY's *tortured body.*

SUZY-BILLY
(*With composure*)

Why are you come?

WALT

Billy—

He goes toward BILLY.

70

ACROSS THE EVERGLADES

SUZY-BILLY
(*Stopping* WALT)
Don't touch Billy. Billy full of poison. My people come. They bury him our way.

WALT
Even the trees are on their side.
He staggers, sinks to his knees.

SUZY-BILLY
(*Helping him rise*)
Come to my boat.

WALT
These stinkin' Glades . . .

DISSOLVE

EVERGLADES PRAIRIE—DAWN
SUZY-BILLY *is poling her dugout toward Miami.* WALT, *semiconscious, is stretched out on the bottom of the boat.*

DISSOLVE

BUZZARD KEY (NEAR LOSTMAN'S RIVER)—DAY
COTTONMOUTH *leads* SLOW-BOY, PERFESSER, WRITER, BEEF, WINDY, ONE-NOTE, SAWDUST *and* LOSER *as they round the point, some carrying rifles and shotguns, others carrying machetes.* BEEF *and* ONE-NOTE *are supporting a huge wild razorback boar on a pole. When they see* MARY MELONS' *ramshackle houseboat tied up with its load of melons piled up on the bow,* WRITER *says:*

WRITER
Hey, look who's here.

PERFESSER
Mary Melons. Salutations, Mary.

COTTONMOUTH
How's yer melons, Mary?

MARY

(*A lusty, female counterpart of* COTTONMOUTH, *shouting back*)
Howdy, Cottonmouth. Why don't yuh come aboard 'n try one?

COTTONMOUTH

Think I will. I'm in the mood fer them nice ripe melons o' yourn.

> COTTONMOUTH *walks up the rickety gangplank as* MARY, *a buxom, good-natured, slatternly woman holds up a melon.*

MARY

Yer always lookin' fer what I'm sellin', ya hungry man.

COTTONMOUTH

Been behavin'?

MARY

Same as usual. Full o' grits, mullet 'n big ideas.

> *From the houseboat* MARY MELONS' *daughter appears with a few more dresses for the clothesline. She is pretty in a wistful, ragged way.*

COTTONMOUTH

Memory, yer gittin' more like your old lady every day.

> *Watching from the foot of the gangplank,* WINDY *is obviously shyly but strongly attracted to* MEMORY. *He climbs aboard the boat to be closer to her. Meanwhile* COTTONMOUTH *is throwing melons down to his crew.*

COTTONMOUTH

Have some melon, boys.

MARY

On my way down through the bay I seen Suzy-Billy headin' that pore bird-warden fella toward Miami.

COTTONMOUTH

Uh-huh.

MARY MELONS

He's so beat-down he's lyin' in the bottom o' the boat too weak t' brush the skeeters off'n his brow.

SAWDUST

Jes' like you figgered, huh, Cottonmouth?

WRITER

All we had t' do was leave 'im t' the mercy of Mother Nature.

BEEF

That's all we hadda do.

COTTONMOUTH

Natural causes. Right, Curley Cue?

He glances toward his pocket.

WINDY *is trying to speak to* MEMORY *in the imaginative, improvised language of the mute. He breaks a melon in two and offers her half of it. Then, meaningfully, he puts the two halves together again.*

WRITER

Hey, I see what he means. He's wantin' t'marry Mary Melons' kid.

ONE-NOTE

I seen him eyein' her every time we come by.

MARY

Memory's shy for fifteen. I was beginnin' t' think I had an old maid on my hands.

COTTONMOUTH

C'n a no-talkin' man do the job?

MARY

Conversation ain't what Memory needs the most of anyway. 'N we been needin' some man-muscles t'do the heavy work. (*To* MEMORY) You willin' to take this man, Memory?

MEMORY *nods and takes* WINDY's *hand.*

COTTONMOUTH

Well, you got him—now hang on to him. Okay, boys. Now git back and skin out that razorback. I'll be there when I git there.

> *All but* SLOW-BOY *start off.* COTTONMOUTH *throws him half a melon.*

MARY

He looks nice 'n healthy.

COTTONMOUTH

I'm takin' good care of 'im. C'mon down inta the cabin, Mary, and I'll settle up with yuh. (*He sucks on his half of the melon, and slaps* MARY *lustily, at the cabin door*) Ah, the sweet-tastin' joys of this world!

> MARY *laughs as they disappear below. On the roof,* WINDY *and* MEMORY, *as casually twained as a pair of mating birds, begin sorting the melons together.*

DISSOLVE

MIAMI—NATHANSON'S STORE—NIGHT

> GEORGE LIGGETT *and* JOE BOTTLES *support* WALT, *barely conscious, between them, as* NAOMI *admits them. She is startled at his ragged, swollen, feverish appearance.*

LIGGETT

We found him lying on the dock. He's in pretty bad shape.

WALT

(*Muttering deliriously*)

Mud 'n mosquitoes. Mud 'n mosquitoes 'n manchineel trees. 'N rivers, hundreds o' rivers, all of 'em Lostman's River . . .

NAOMI

(*Leading the way*)

Follow me. I'll show you where to put him. (*She leads them down the hall to* WALT's *room*) In here, Mr. Liggett.

74

LIGGETT *and* JOE BOTTLES *carry him inside.* NAOMI *leans her head against the door for a moment.* LIGGETT *comes out.*

LIGGETT
(*Both solicitous and self-satisfied*)

Looks like he's had his fill of the Glades. If he has any brains he'll settle down here in town and find himself a wife. Don't you think so, Miss Naomi?

NAOMI

Tell Dr. Coggin we need him right away.

LIGGETT

Yes, ma'am.

He goes out, followed by JOE BOTTLES. NAOMI *turns toward the room where* WALT *is groaning deliriously.*

NAOMI

Poppa! Poppa!

Her father hurries down the hall to help NAOMI.

DISSOLVE

NATHANSON'S SITTING ROOM—A WEEK LATER

NAOMI *is playing a gay hit song of the day on her player piano. Suddenly there is a piercing scream from* WALT, *who is lying on the couch.* NAOMI *jumps up and goes to him.*

WALT
(*Awakening from a nightmare*)

The piano—the piano. What's it doing here in the mangrove swamp?

NAOMI

You just asked me to play it for you.

75

WALT
(*Coming to*)

Oh—guess I must have dozed off. I was dreaming of a man-chineel tree growing right up out of a piano—and you were—

NAOMI

Don't try to tell me the dream. Our piano isn't in the Glades. It's right here in the parlor. Oh, how I pestered Poppa for that player piano! He says it isn't lady-like to be so persistent.

WALT

What was that song you were just playing?

NAOMI

It's a new rag-time version of "Yankee Doodle Went to Town."

NATHANSON *enters, carrying a breakfast tray which he sets down on* WALT's *lap.*

NATHANSON
(*Singing*)

"Yankee Doodle went to town
Riding on his pony
Stuck a feather in his hat . . ."

But that was before the Audubon Society. (*They hear the sound of an oncoming train*) The Miami Special. (*Looking at his watch*) Almost on time.

WALT

Is this Monday?

NATHANSON

Thursday. Things have been humming while you were away. We have two trains a week now. We're dredging the river for bigger boats. Liggett is just finishing a new warehouse and I've been building an addition to the store. You didn't know I was a carpenter, did you? I didn't either until I had to build this place with my own hands. But two hands aren't enough any more. I need you with me, son. With your knowledge of the Everglades and my plan for cutting the canals, clearing the palmetto—

NAOMI

Poppa—

NATHANSON

I know—I know. No more speeches, Poppa. Now eat, rest, listen to Naomi's "restful" music—rag-time she likes, and I raised her on Chopin and Mendelssohn.

He exits.

WALT

You have a wonderful father.

NAOMI

Poppa's quite a fellow. Now lie back and rest. We've got to get you on your feet for the Fourth of July.

DISSOLVE

FOURTH OF JULY PICNIC—BEACH ON KEY BIS-CAYNE—DAY

On the bandstand, JUDGE TIPPINS *is being congratulated by the bandleader on the speech he has just finished some minutes ago. The* JUDGE *asks the bandleader to honor him by sharing a drink from his bottle. Then the* JUDGE *comes down from the bandstand toward the long buffet table, stocked with tureens of turtle soup and other festive tropical delicacies.* GEORGE LIGGETT *is telling the* MAYOR *and other officials that* JUDGE TIPPINS *will certainly be the next governor.* NATHANSON *and* MORGAN, *their plates full, are headed for their private picnic area, close to the water's edge.*

Several small children, in quaint white knickers and

77

long party dresses, are toasting marshmallows, while others are setting off firecrackers.

MRS. BRADFORD'S *boat, "Star of the Everglades," is sailing near the shore—all her lovely girls aboard, drinking champagne and waving little American flags at the crowd, some of whom, in the ludicrously copious black bathing suits of the day, are dunking themselves in the water.*

NATHANSON *and* MORGAN *join their friends, who are already seated around a picnic spread of crawfish, tropical fruit and wine. Behind them, in the surf,* NAOMI *is bathing, while* WALT, *now fully recovered, is picking up shells.*

NATHANSON

I think of myself as a good American but someday someone will have to explain to me why we celebrate the signing of the Declaration of Independence—a glorious document—a solemn occasion with small boys devoting their day to making the loudest noises they can think of. (*At that moment a firecracker explodes not far from* NATHANSON. *The boy who has thrown it turns and scampers off.* NATHANSON *calls after him*) But don't stop. I like it.

NAOMI *comes running up toward them out of the water wearing a wet and—for the period—daring sheath bathing suit.* WALT *follows her, in rolled-up flannels, barefoot, his shirt open. He is carrying some conch shells he has taken from the shallow water.*

NAOMI

The water is wonderful, Poppa. You should go for a swim.

NATHANSON

Next year maybe you can convince me it's proper for the host to wear a bathing suit in front of his guests.

ACROSS THE EVERGLADES

NAOMI

Oh, Poppa, you're so old-fashioned.

WALT

(*Opening shells*)

Conchs. Fresh out of the sea. This is better than the Waldorf.

NAOMI

Poppa, every year you say next year. (*To* WALT) Can you imagine, he didn't even want me to wear my new bathing suit. He said it's too daring—too shocking.

NATHANSON

I knew the moment she saw the new sheath style in *Harper's* she would sit right down and copy it. Incorrigible!

NAOMI

Has Walt complained about it?

WALT

Walt likes it.

NATHANSON

This modern generation—sheath bathing suits—the bunny hug—fast motorcars—what are they coming to?

MORGAN

The eternal protest of every aging generation.

NATHANSON

(*Looking at* NAOMI *and smiling*)

You're right, Ross, it's not the changing styles that matter, it's the human heart inside the sheath.

WALT

While you gentlemen are philosophizing, this materialist may be finishing off the conchs.

At this moment, JUDGE TIPPINS *and his wife approach.*

JUDGE TIPPINS

Good afternoon, Aaron. Happy Independence Day! (*The* JUDGE *is now a little tipsy*) A heavenly day for our celebration.

NATHANSON

Hello, your Honor, I think your speech at the ceremony was even better than last year.

JUDGE TIPPINS

(*Modestly*)

I do what I can to imbue my fellow citizens with the proper patriotic spirit—(*Eagerly accepts a drink from* NATHANSON) Thank you. Don't mind if I do.

WOMAN GUEST

I think when you said "verily the red, white and blue is all around us this afternoon" that was absolutely inspiring. That's such a charming word—"verily."

JUDGE TIPPINS

Madame, I'm delighted that you appreciate the romance of language. And as I was saying only a very short while ago "verily the red, white and blue is all around us this glorious afternoon and I am reminded . . ."

> *The* JUDGE *is obviously warming up to a flowery repetition of the speech he has already given, somewhat to* NATHANSON's *chagrin.*

NAOMI

(*Sotto voce to* WALT)

Every Fourth of July he goes down the beach repeating the same old speech.

WALT

I'm a patriot, but the only trouble with patriotism is politicians.

NAOMI

I just feel like running down the beach.

Impulsively WALT *and* NAOMI *get up and dart off down the beach together, leaving the* JUDGE *to continue his oration. From her boat,* MRS. BRADFORD *waves and calls to him.*

MRS. BRADFORD

Congratulations, Judge. A glorious speech! A glorious day! A glorious occasion!

She lifts her champagne glass toward him.

JUDGE TIPPINS

Thank you, thank you, madame.

MRS. TIPPINS

Isn't that the notorious Mrs. Bradford?

JUDGE TIPPINS

Hmm. Yes, I think it is.

MRS. TIPPINS

Marshfield, as one of the leaders of this community you ought to be able to do something about that brazen woman.

JUDGE TIPPINS

(*Righteously*)

I'm doing everything I can. (*He steals a glance at the irrepressible* MRS. BRADFORD. *Then, catching himself*) Ladies and Gentlemen, if you will excuse us, we'll continue our promenade.

They leave in the direction of LIGGETT's *picnic group a little farther down the beach. This is an elaborate affair.* LIGGETT *is seated at the head of the table, his top hat royally on his head, pouring champagne for his guests.*

MRS. BRADFORD

(*From the gaily festooned bow of her boat*)
Yoo hoo! Georgie! Yoo hoo!

MRS. LIGGETT

Are those hussies calling you, George?

LIGGETT

Er—er—impossible, my pet. After all, George is a very common name.

> *He laughs nervously.* WALT *and* NAOMI *are running past them in the background. They reach an upturned rowboat on the bank of a small lagoon.* NAOMI *lies back on it and looks up at the sky.* WALT *sits close to her. A roseate spoonbill feeds peacefully in the shallows nearby.*

WALT

A roseate spoonbill. He likes to get off by himself. An individualist. A sort of gentleman philosopher.

NAOMI

He is beautiful.

WALT

The size of him. The special color of his wings. The funny way he feeds.

NAOMI

What made you so interested in birds?

WALT

My father. He was a funny guy. Came off a farm in upstate New York. My mother was a city girl from Buffalo. They met when she came out to the country one summer. He settled down in the city to please her. Tried all kinds of businesses—luggage, hardware, a candy store—a whole string of little stores that kept going under. When the sun was going down—just about this time—he used to take me walking in the park. Do you know there are ninety-three different kinds of birds in that park? By the time I was twelve I could tell a scarlet tanager from a cardinal a hundred feet away. The day the candy store went broke, my old man took me on a long walk out into the country. "Son, I'm a flop. I'm a failure," he kept saying. "I'm a flop. I'm a failure." We walked all day. I saw a big bird I had never seen before. "That's a yellow-crowned night heron," my old man said, and he told me about their migration patterns all the way from Maine to the Caribbean. What he said was, "They've made a perfect adjustment to their environment except for one thing—the interference of man." It's funny, I can still hear him—that's exactly what he said. (*Breaks off*) My poor father, all the time when he should have been out on a farm or in the woods, close to nature, he was going broke trying to sell suitcases or pocket knives or Tootsie-Rolls.

NAOMI
(*Moved*)
What finally happened to him?

WALT
(*With a touch of resentment*)
Nothing. That's what finally happened to him. Nothing. He just died. A job like this one I've been trying to do would've suited him fine. (*Rises, embarrassed, and quickly changes the subject*) Come on, I'll race you to the bandstand.

NAOMI
You're getting ready to go back.

WALT
I guess so. Back to those damned snakes and the heat and the mud and the bugs. How could I ever have thought it was beautiful?

NAOMI

You men—forever confusing beauty and danger. It's men who are the hopeless romantics. It's women who are the down-to-earth realists.

WALT

But to have to face yourself and admit you aren't strong enough to do something you set out to do.

NAOMI

Men make me furious sometimes. So possessive of your precious male courage—like little boys playing games trying to prove how brave you are. Did you ever stop to think—I wonder how brave Columbus seemed to his own family—Behind every one of those brave explorers there's a forgotten family. Or like Gauguin bravely giving up his wife and seven children for his art and his native girls in the South Seas.

WALT

Look, Naomi, I'm not trying to be a trail-blazer, a world-saver, but there'll always be a need for men who can—

NAOMI

Oh, you men! You heroes! Striking dramatic poses. You're all the same—self-indulgent, irresponsible Don Quixotes, chasing windmills.

WALT

Listen, Naomi—those aren't windmills—

NAOMI

I'd even rather listen to the Judge.

> *She runs away in the direction of the bandstand.* WALT *follows just as she reaches the bandstand,* WALT *catches up to her, takes her in his arms, and kisses her. She responds.*

WALT

I've been wanting to do this for a long time.

NAOMI
(*Breathlessly*)

I know. I know.

He kisses her again, and draws her into a covered space about four feet high under the bandstand.

WALT

I love your mouth. I watch it all the time. Your funny wide mouth.

NAOMI

Stay with me.

WALT

Yes.

NAOMI

Tonight.

WALT
(*Kissing her*)

Yes.

NAOMI

Tomorrow.

WALT

Yes.

NAOMI

How many tomorrows?

WALT

How many do you want?

NAOMI

All of them. Give me every last one of them. I'm a give-me, give-me, greedy girl.

WALT

I give them to you. I'm ready to give them to you.

NAOMI

I wasn't jealous of Mrs. Bradford's girls, I was jealous of those birds. Imagine having 40,000 rivals. (*Then, more seri-*

ously) There are all kinds of conservation. Conservation of peoples, for instance. I want you to conserve us, Walt and Naomi. (*Embracing him*) Oh, I love you in such a shameless, private under-the-bandstand way.

WALT

You know, you're the boldest girl I ever met. Bold and refined—a devastating combination.

NAOMI

I like devastated men.

> *Up above them the band begins to assemble and tune up with dissonant blasts.*

NAOMI

Oh, the band concert. In ten minutes we'll be surrounded.

WALT

Let's hurry back to town. We'll have it all to ourselves.

> *They look at each other and run off, hand in hand.*

DISSOLVE

FLAGLER STREET—MIAMI—DAY

> *The opening of a new extension of this unpaved thoroughfare is being dedicated. The road goes "nowhere," leading to the tropical jungle growth that lies beyond the boundaries of the frontier town. A band of red bunting is stretched across the street, held by two pretty girls, one on each side. One of the girls is* NAOMI. *A motorcade of resplendent vehicles of the 1905–1910 period, conveying important personages of the town, heads toward the bunting. In front is* GEORGE LIGGETT'S *Cadillac, carrying* LIGGETT *and his wife, who is wearing the same spectacular egret feathers in her hat; also in the car are the* MAYOR *and his wife and the chairman of the State Improvement Commission. The second car*

carries JUDGE TIPPINS *and* MRS. TIPPINS, MORGAN *and* NATHANSON. *The sirens are sounding, the bells are clanging. Some hundred fancily dressed onlookers applaud and whistle.*

WALT *is standing near* NAOMI *as the last vehicle of the motorcade approaches. When he sees* MRS. LIGGETT'S *hat his old resentment flares for a moment, but he looks at* NAOMI *reassuringly, as if to say, "Don't worry. I promised you to settle down and give up the Glades and the feather fight." He seems citified, subdued, tamed. He approaches* NATHANSON'S *car.*

NATHANSON
(*To* WALT, *exhilarated*)

Think of it, Flagler Street half a mile long. Your survey on the manchineel and poison-tree problem has been a great help to this project.

WALT

I don't think I'll forget a manchineel.

NATHANSON

I know people think I'm crazy, but one of these days you'll be able to drive two miles along Flagler Street—pavement all the way.

WALT

I'm not against paving Flagler Street.

NATHANSON

Look at Liggett soft-soaping those Improvement Commissioners. I think our report will talk louder than his words of honey at the drainage hearing this afternoon.

WALT

Three o'clock at City Hall?

NATHANSON

Right. We go on after Liggett. (*Turns to* NAOMI, *confidently*) We'll make a civic leader out of him yet.

WALT

I'll go and collect my papers and be there on time.

> *The motorcade drives on.* WALT *heads toward the docks.*

DISSOLVE

LIGGETT'S WAREHOUSE FACING DOCK—DAY

> WALT *has picked up his papers, is carrying a briefcase, and is about to mount his bicycle when he sees* MARY MELONS *and* WINDY *in her skiff, tied up at the dock. Being lifted by* WINDY *and some Negro dock workers on a thick mattress is* SAWDUST. *In charge is* LIGGETT'S *English clerk.* SAWDUST *groans slightly, with his eyes closed. The weight of the mattress bearing the limp* SAWDUST *is clumsy to handle, and the Negroes almost lose their grasp on it for a moment. Inadvertently* SAWDUST *glances nervously at the water below him.* WALT *recognizes him and approaches.*

WALT

What's the matter with him?

MARY MELONS

He's got the dangy fever. The pore fella's more dead than alive.

> SAWDUST *moans piteously.*

ENGLISHMAN

I'm sure Mr. Liggett won't mind if we make the poor man comfortable in our warehouse. I'll send for a doctor immediately.

WALT

(*To* SAWDUST, *suspiciously*)

Dengue fever, eh? I know a little about that. Are your bones aching?

SAWDUST

(*Weakly*)

My neck—it's all stiffed up. I can't move my head.

WALT

That's funny. You didn't seem to have any trouble moving it a minute ago.

> *Intuitively,* WALT *whips out a pocket knife and plunges it downward into the mattress.* SAWDUST *bolts from the mattress, unleashing the long circus whip he was holding under him.* WALT's *knife makes a foot-long gash in the mattress revealing it to be stuffed with precious plumes —white egret, blue heron, pink and carmine spoonbill.* MARY MELONS *and* WINDY *have grabbed* SAWDUST.

MARY

Get back into the boat, Sawdust, before I stomp your head in.

> *They hurriedly drag him into the boat and cast off.*

WALT

(*To the Negro dockers, purposefully*)

Hang on to this mattress and follow me.

DISSOLVE

COURTROOM—MIAMI CITY HALL—DAY

> *The drainage hearing is in session. The Commissioners, on the rostrum, are listening to* LIGGETT, *completing his presentation. In the front row, listening intently, are* NATHANSON *and* NAOMI, *among some twenty townspeople crowded into the small meeting room.*

LIGGETT

And so, if I am given the franchise, I will be prepared to issue stock and to put on the market two hundred and fifty thousand acres at thirty dollars—

At the back of the hall, WALT *appears with the Negroes carrying the mattress.*

WALT

Mr. Liggett, I charge you with illegally receiving at least twenty thousand dollars' worth of plumes—and here's the evidence—

He slashes the mattress from one end to the other. The valuable plumes pour out onto the floor. Spectators spring to their feet. Everyone is talking at once. The chairman pounds his gavel for quiet.

WALT

(*Brandishing a fistful of feathers in his hand*)

Under the law of this State, I'm confiscating this entire shipment and ask that warrants be issued for the men who brought it in.

LIGGETT

(*Furiously*)

I thought you had given up all that foolishness—now that you've become a partner of Nathanson's.

WALT

I thought so too. But a shipment like this means wiping out a whole thriving rookery.

LIGGETT

(*Turning to Commissioners*)

Gentlemen, I protest. Everyone knows Nathanson and I are bucking each other for the drainage franchise. They also know this young busy-body is about to become his son-in-law. Can't you see what they're doing? It's just a sneaky immigrant trick to discredit me in the eyes of this Commission.

Spectators look from LIGGETT *to* NATHANSON. *Some seem to side with one, some with the other.* NATHANSON *is mortified.* JUDGE TIPPINS *speaks.*

JUDGE TIPPINS

Young man, are you ready to press formal charges against Mr. Liggett?

WALT

I am, your Honor.

JUDGE TIPPINS

Mr. Liggett, consider yourself in technical custody to appear in this court at half past nine tomorrow morning to answer the charges.

WALT

Thank you, your Honor.

LIGGETT

Of course, your Honor. (*Then, pointing to* NATHANSON) But isn't it obvious he's in cahoots with his future son-in-law to gyp me out of the franchise?

COMMISSION CHAIRMAN

That will do, Mr. Liggett. Now, Mr. Nathanson, we will hear your presentation.

NATHANSON *rises, then he hears:*

A SPECTATOR

Sit down, foreigner.

A number of spectators join in the heckling; others demand that NATHANSON *be heard.* WALT, *who was about to leave, turns back into the hall.*

NATHANSON

Gentlemen of the Commission, I've spent years building a spotless reputation in this town. I was accepted as an equal, a fellow-pioneer. There wasn't a whisper of sharp dealing or prejudice.

2ND SPECTATOR

Sit down!

JUDGE
(*Banging gavel*)

Order! Order!

NATHANSON

Under these unfortunate circumstances I prefer to postpone my application. I've learned how to wait—so I'll wait a little longer.

Putting his thick report back into his briefcase, NATHANSON *exits with* NAOMI. *People make way for him, some of them obviously critical.*

DISSOLVE

NATHANSON'S STORE—NEXT MORNING

As WALT *enters from the stairway with his briefcase, on his way to* LIGGETT'S *arraignment, he finds* NAOMI *standing forlornly in the empty, shuttered store.* NATHANSON *is on the balcony putting up the last shutters.*

WALT

It's only nine o'clock. Why is Aaron closing the store?

NAOMI

He's too proud to leave his store open to anyone who might believe Liggett's lies.

WALT

I'm sorry, Naomi. But isn't he taking it a little hard? After all, Liggett is an old wind-bag. Sure he'll get a few narrow-minded people to agree with him, but—

NATHANSON *enters abruptly from the balcony, bolting the door behind him.*

NATHANSON

Maybe you've got to see what we've seen to understand. That man, the same enemy who's plagued us for 5,000 years, is going around town spreading viciousness about me—those same old lies.

WALT

Aaron—

NATHANSON

You don't know—but we do—this is the way it always begins. Some bully puts you on the defensive—and you act defensive—then you're ashamed of being defensive and you act ashamed—that makes you different. And the next thing you know, instead of people saying, "There's Aaron Nathanson, he's one of us," they're saying, "There's Aaron Nathanson, he's different from us." Excuse me.

And NATHANSON *exits to rear of store.*

WALT

I wish there were something I could do.

NAOMI

There is. If you were to drop the charges against Liggett.

WALT

Naomi—

NAOMI

I know that's hard for you. But if it's the only thing that will stop Liggett from spreading his filthy racial poison . . .

WALT

I'm due there at nine-thirty.

Troubled, torn between his Audubon responsibility and his desire to ease the tension on AARON NATHANSON, WALT *unbolts the front door and goes out.* NAOMI *bolts it after him. She, too, is troubled by having asked* WALT *to reverse himself on a matter of conscience.*

DISSOLVE

MIAMI COURTROOM—DAY

JUDGE TIPPINS is presiding. LIGGETT is accompanied by his lawyer. Spectators crowd the room. WALT sits nervously next to MORGAN. NAOMI slips in and stands at the rear.

JUDGE TIPPINS

Mr. Murdock, you will please take the witness stand and repeat under oath your charges against the defendant George Liggett.

WALT
(Rising reluctantly, struggling against himself)

Your Honor, on further inspection . . . I find the evidence against Mr. Liggett inconclusive. I . . . wish to drop my charges at this time.

There is an excited murmuring from the spectators. NAOMI lowers her head. MORGAN stares at WALT in shocked anger as the latter walks toward the entrance.

WALT
(Taking leave, shaken)

Your Honor—Mr. Liggett.

LIGGETT grabs his arm as WALT is about to exit.

LIGGETT

Son, I thought you'd come to your senses. You're gonna learn to live with this town.

WALT
(Edgy)

Will I?

WALT walks out.

LIGGETT

He'll be all right.

OUTSIDE THE COURTHOUSE

As MORGAN angrily follows the crestfallen WALT.

MORGAN

I'm disgusted with you. One of these days we're going to get a warden who'll stand up and fight the Liggetts and the Cottonmouths to a finish. I'm wiring Tallahassee to revoke your commission.

WALT *cannot answer. He walks on, toward the river-front.*

DISSOLVE

MRS. BRADFORD'S—THAT NIGHT

The place is almost deserted. Several of the girls sit at tables alone, smoking and drinking forlornly. MRS. BRADFORD *sits in an alcove in the rear, eyeglasses on her nose, a fashionable quill pen in her hand, going over her ledger.* JOE BOTTLES *is at the bar, in his cups, talking quietly with the bartender. The piano player sings and chords a slow, haunting blues.* WALT *enters. He has been walking the night, trying to reach a difficult decision.*

WALT

(*To* MRS. BRADFORD)

Slow night?

MRS. BRADFORD

Once in a while I welcome a slow night—gives me a chance to catch up on my books and drop my southern accent. Mr. Liggett was in earlier enjoying a little private celebration—you play ball with him like you did today and I know you two are gonna wind up being friends.

WALT *crosses to the piano player and moodily listens awhile to "Lonely Boy Blues." Then he goes back to the bar where* JOE BOTTLES *and the bartender are talking.*

JOE BOTTLES

Hope the weather breaks enough for me to shove off in the mornin'.

BARTENDER

Where you fixin' to go this time, Joe?

JOE BOTTLES

Oh, Key Largo—Bottle Key—Flamingo. If the weather holds I'll run over as far as Cape Sable.

WALT

That's not too far from Cottonmouth Key.

JOE

Maybe another thirty-five miles.

WALT

Do you take any passengers?

JOE

I'll do anything for anybody—if there's money in it. You fig'rin' on comin' along?

WALT

I don't know. Let me think about it.

JOE

Go ahead, think all you want. If a nor'wester don't break, I'm castin' off with the first crack o' dawn. If you come aboard with twenty-five green ones in hand, fine 'n dandy. If not, well, can't say I'd blame you none.

WALT

Sometimes I wish I was a drifter like you, Joe. Life'd be simpler. Let me think about it.

WALT *puts a coin on the table, finishes his drink and exits.*

DISSOLVE

DESERTED DOCK ON MIAMI RIVER—NEXT MORNING

WALT *sits on a weathered piling and stares into the river. Close by,* JOE BOTTLES *is on his sloop preparing to*

cast off. A mullet fisherman passes in a skiff loaded with
fish to the gunnels.

FISHERMAN

Howdy, Walt. The mullet was thick as skeeters out there
this mornin'.

WALT *nods, preoccupied.* NAOMI *comes up to him.*

NAOMI

Thank you, for yesterday. (WALT *doesn't answer*) I know
how difficult it was.

WALT

It was. It still is.

He stares off at JOE BOTTLES' *sloop. She follows his look.*

NAOMI

You're going back.

WALT

Are you giving me any choice?

NAOMI

I—suppose not.

JOE BOTTLES

Yuh comin' or ain'tcha?

WALT

Naomi, I think I should marry you before I go.

NAOMI

I don't want you to marry me—as a favor—a gesture to
respectability.

WALT

No—I'd marry you for a better reason.

NAOMI

Don't worry. I'll take care of myself. I've learned to take
care of myself. (*From around her neck she removes a golden
Star of David and places it over* WALT's *head*) This helped us
through many dangers.

97

Instead of sobbing and throwing herself into his arms, as she feels compelled to do, she turns, dry-eyed, and hurries from the river. WALT *watches her until she disappears. Then he runs along the dock toward* JOE BOTTLES' *sloop and jumps aboard.* JOE *casts off.*

DISSOLVE

JOE BOTTLES' SLOOP—DAWN
With WALT *aboard, heading down Miami Bay.*

DISSOLVE

THE SLOOP—LATER THAT MORNING
Somewhere along the upper Keys.

DISSOLVE

SLOOP OFF CAPE SABLE—AFTERNOON
The wind is blowing harder. A brooding purple sky heralds a tropical storm.

DISSOLVE

THE SLOOP IN THE STORM
They are lashed by a hurricane blow and a tropical downpour.

DISSOLVE

NEAR SHORE OF COTTONMOUTH KEY—NIGHT
It is still pouring. JOE BOTTLES *is tying up the "Sick Pelican," his sloop.* WALT *is lowering a small skiff into the water.*

JOE BOTTLES
(Reaching for his jug)
There it is. Maybe you'd better take another pull on this. (WALT *does so and climbs into the small boat. Tossing the empty jug away,* JOE *follows, and they head toward shore*) Least you're lucky ya got the wind with ya. Mebbe he won't hear ya comin'.

They can hear, coming from the cook shack, and muffled by the wind, the sound of wild laughter and country music. Their little skiff fights the rough waters on its way toward shore.

WALT
(*Peering ahead*)
Cottonmouth Key—its own world. (*Taking out gun*) I'll pay you for this when I get back to Miami.

JOE BOTTLES
If you don't make it back, I'll collect when they auction off your gear.

WALT
(*Tense*)
You're a cheerful cuss.

COTTONMOUTH KEY—NIGHT

In the cook shack, COTTONMOUTH sits drinking, playing with his snake, and overlooking his gang, who are grouped around a large table, playing cards. ONE-NOTE is playing his guitar, with several of the boys chiming in raucously. The storm makes the shack creak. On the table the food is plentiful—venison, ibis, 'gator steak, wild turkey, turtle. SLOW-BOY sits next to COTTONMOUTH, with his pet coon on his shoulder.

As the card-playing, singing and drinking continue, COTTONMOUTH's animal senses alert him to something. He rises, gives the snake to SLOW-BOY, jumps down from the shack, and strides silently toward the bank.

As WALT climbs ashore, followed by JOE BOTTLES, COTTONMOUTH is standing in the shadows of the alligator pen, waiting for him. He reaches out, surprising WALT, and snatches his gun away.

99

COTTONMOUTH

Yuh lookin' fer me?

WALT

I was.

COTTONMOUTH

Y'know, I'm glad to see yuh. I was beginnin' t'think yuh never was gonna git here. (*To* JOE BOTTLES) Joe, how much didya nick 'im for guidin' 'im in?

JOE BOTTLES
(*Nervously*)

Twenty-five mainline.

COTTONMOUTH

I'da paid yuh twice that much t'bring 'im in. Come in outa the blow.

COTTONMOUTH *leads them to the cook shack where the gang is waiting to see what* COTTONMOUTH *is bringing in.*

COTTONMOUTH
(*To his gang*)

Boys, I want yuh t' behave yerselves now—we got company.

PERFESSER

An official invitation?

SAWDUST

Yeah, who ast 'im?

BEEF

Not me.

COTTONMOUTH

Mebbe Curley Cue asked 'im.

COTTONMOUTH *flings the snake toward* WALT, *who instinctively grabs it and hurls it violently to the ground. The snake lies dead.* WALT *waits with a kind of aroused resignation. All the men watch* COTTONMOUTH *to see what he will do.*

COTTONMOUTH

Curley Cue was the best friend I had around here. He has a better chance o' meetin' his Maker than most of you reptiles.

BIGAMY BOB

God have mercy on yer blasphemy. I've got the faith.

COTTONMOUTH

With seven wives at one time yuh gotta have faith. (*A powerful gust of wind hits the shack with tremendous force, blowing the cards in all directions*) It's comin'. Let's move this little party into the shack.

The squatters quickly collect the food and jugs and start following COTTONMOUTH *toward his shack.*

JOE BOTTLES

(*To* COTTONMOUTH)

Mind if I move my boat up the river?

COTTONMOUTH

Go ahead. (*Giving him a playful boot*) I'll be seein' ya.

JOE BOTTLES *heads for the skiff as fast as the wind will allow him.*

SAWDUST

(*Heading for the shack*)

Don't forget the jug.

LOSER

Ferget it? It's my best friend.

WRITER

Nothing like a blow to bring on a thirst.

PERFESSER

An ideal night for libation.

They laugh and shout back at the wild night as they hurry into COTTONMOUTH's *shack.* COTTONMOUTH *prods* WALT *forward with the butt of his rifle.*

INSIDE COTTONMOUTH'S SHACK—NIGHT

> COTTONMOUTH's *great black bear of a chair is pulled up to a crude outsized round table. On the walls are shotguns and hunting trophies, panther and otter, giant rattlesnake and 'gator skins. A table near the stove is laden with game, fried ibis and blue heron, wildcat and 'gator steaks, roast wild turkeys. The large, rough, but homey shack creaks on its stilts but stands firm against the wind that howls outside. The men group themselves around* WALT *menacingly, jibing at him with vicious humor.*

VARIOUS PLUME HUNTERS

Maybe we better open a shutter. Something stinks in here. We're gonna have a party, a nice little necktie party for Bird-Boy.

We got a new dish on the menu, cooked Bird-Boy.

PERFESSER

We got him in our parlor now.

> *They all move in on* WALT, *who eyes them like a cornered animal. But* COTTONMOUTH, *simply by clearing his throat, relieves the tension—at least momentarily.*

COTTONMOUTH

Seein' as how none of us ain't goin' noplace, le's make like he's droppin' in friendly. (COTTONMOUTH *is relaxed and jovial. The rest of the squatters are restive and suspicious*) Ye're glad t'see 'im, git the idea? Smile on 'im. (*Seeing their grim looks*) I said *smile.* (*Nothing happens*) When I say smile—(*Stiffly, self-consciously, and not too successfully,* COTTONMOUTH's "army" *try to light their disreputable faces with smiles of hospitality. They squeeze their faces into evil, Daumier-like caricatures of human warmth*) That's better.

> *Outside the storm mounts, shaking the shack to its rickety foundations.*

COTTONMOUTH

(*To* WALT, *indicating a chair at the opposite side of the table*)
Sit down, boy. Have some snake medicine.

WALT

(*On his guard, but accepting the jug* COTTONMOUTH *pushes to him*)
Cottonmouth, I must say you're a gentleman. (*Drinks and pushes the jug back across the table*)
> COTTONMOUTH *takes another swig and then pushes the jug back again to* WALT. WALT *drinks again and shoves the jug back toward* COTTONMOUTH. WRITER *reaches for it but* COTTONMOUTH *knocks his hand away.*

COTTONMOUTH

Wait a minute. We's drinkin' together.

WRITER

Oh—the dyin' man drank a hearty breakfast.
> COTTONMOUTH *pushes the jug to* WALT, *who takes another swig.*

LOSER

He was a livin' dead-man when he walked in here.

PERFESSER

Cottonmouth, seein' as how an unpleasant little detail would seem to be indicated here, why don't we all draw straws to see who assumes the unfortunate reponsibility? Wouldn't that be the fair and democratic way?

WRITER

A knife may not be so democratic, but it's a lot quicker.

SAWDUST

Give 'im to me, boss—I'll bury him alive.

COTTONMOUTH

Shut up! It's too splashin' wet outside to bury a man tonight. This ain't no night for killin'. Hell, it ain't every night we git t'entertain a good-lookin' eddicated stranger. Boys, go put your snouts in the trough. One-Note, I wanna hear it again—*Lostman's River*.

ONE-NOTE

You got it comin', Cottonmouth—*Lostman's River*.

>ONE-NOTE *sings and plays a local favorite, "If I could be an alligator, I'd wrap my tail around your neck . . ." The squatters help themselves to the plenteous food.* WALT *and* COTTONMOUTH *go on drinking, their eyes fixed on each other.*

DISSOLVE

>*Sometime later. The rain is still coming down. The squatters have eaten and drunk extensively. Several have passed out.* WALT *seems to have drunk himself into obliviousness of danger. He joins in the singing of another ballad.* SLOW-BOY *comes in from the porch with a small snake he takes to his father.*

SLOW-BOY

Here's a new young-un we kin raise as a pet.

COTTONMOUTH
(*Taking it*)
Now didn't yuh pick out a nice lil one, boy. Much obliged.

SLOW-BOY

I saw the Devil out there in the lean-to. (SAWDUST *starts to laugh*) He was drinkin' from one o' these here jugs 'n I had to yank it away from 'im. Honest I did.

COTTONMOUTH

What'd the old Devil look like, boy?

SLOW-BOY

Well—he—now don't git mad, Paw—he looked kinda like you—dressed kinda the same 'n he had red hair curlin' right around his horns.

SAWDUST

Around his horns . . .

They all laugh at SLOW-BOY *except* COTTONMOUTH.

COTTONMOUTH

(*Sharply commanding*)

Stop laughing! (*To* SLOW-BOY) Course ye did, son. (*To* ONE-NOTE) Keep a-playin'. (*To* WALT—*after swigging from new jug*) Your turn, Bird-Boy.

WALT

(*Grabbing the jug and slamming it down on the table*)

I'm not a bird and I'm not a boy. The name's Murdock—Walt Murdock.

COTTONMOUTH

(*Half amused, half impressed by* WALT'S *audacity*)

Have a cigar, *Mister* Murdock. (*He hands a cigar to* WALT, *who takes it and lights it up*) Boys, I want you all to make the acquaintance of Mr. Walt Murdock.

At COTTONMOUTH'S *command, the squatters rouse themselves from their various recumbent positions and march around the table, bowing and shaking* WALT'S *hand with mock formality.* COTTONMOUTH *enjoys the sport at* WALT'S *expense. Then he grows more serious.*

COTTONMOUTH

Now, Mr. Murdock, yuh don't see me goin' inta Miamuh and messin' up yer town folks, d'yuh?

WALT

No, Mr. Cottonmouth. What about your messin' up the Glades?

COTTONMOUTH

Sure, I kill the birds 'n the birds kill the fish 'n someday mebbe somethin'll kill me 'n eat me too.

WALT

(*With conviction piercing the alcoholic haze*)

Now listen, Cottonmouth, I know a little something about the balance of nature. I know fish, birds, snakes—including you —have to eat each other to keep that balance, but wiping out whole rookeries, tens of thousands of birds, with twelve-gauge shotguns for easy money, silly fads and fat profits—that's got nothing to do with the balance of nature. That's just greed and destruction.

COTTONMOUTH

You talk mighty pretty. I ought to keep you aroun' here jes t'talk back t' me onct in a while. It's as good as shine fer stirrin' up the blood in a man.

WALT

Might as well say what I think. I've got nothing to lose.

COTTONMOUTH

That's right. Jes' yer life. 'N you must hold that pretty cheap t' come back at me a second time.

WALT

(*Indicating huge pot boiling on stove*)

But at least I don't eat feathers. (*He gets up and goes to the stove, lifting pot cover*) How many feathers you got in that pot, Cottonmouth? How many blue herons and snowy egrets did it take to make that stew? (*Turns to the squatters and shouts*) Hey, you swampies, what do boiled feathers taste like, hm? Tell me!

The squatters rush at WALT *and start to rough him up. In his moonshine euphoria,* WALT *seems to welcome the battle.*

106

COTTONMOUTH

Leave him be! (*To* WALT) Yer fallin' into bad company, boy, I'm over here. Sit down. Have some more shine.

WALT *comes forward and sits down again, helping himself to another drink from the jug.*

COTTONMOUTH

We don't need yer ten commandments in the Glades. We do all right on one. Eat or be et. Eat or be et is the law of the Glades.

PERFESSER

(*Staggering*)

In other words, Cottonmouth carries the freedom of the individual to its logical conclusion.

COTTONMOUTH

Perfesser, here's a knife t'pick them fancy words outa yer teeth. I mean the few yuh got left.

The jug has been making the rounds while ONE-NOTE *has medleyed into another lusty local song.*

Increasingly 'shined and falling into the wildly pervasive away-from-it-all mood, WALT *chimes in on a verse.*

COTTONMOUTH

Walt, ya fit in with these swamp rats pretty good.

WALT

'S beautiful song! (*Sings a few lines alone*)

". . . love 'er like a rose,

How I love that woman, ain't nobody knows!"

COTTONMOUTH

(*Offering a great slab of meat on end of knife*)

Grab yo'self a hunk o' fresh meat.

WALT
(*Munching it*)
Tastes pretty good. What is it?

COTTONMOUTH
'Gator tail.

WALT
Bush-lightning and 'gator. Bring on the Great Flood!

COTTONMOUTH
Ah, the sweet tastin' joys of this world. Now mebbe you can see why we hole out here—

WALT
(*Increasingly under the spell of the head-spinning Cotton-mouth brew*)
No worries, no 'sponsibilities—wild as all the rest of the wildlife. I begin to see what you got here.

COTTONMOUTH
Perfesser, what's that six-bit word yuh got fer the reason we live out here.

PERFESSER
(*With drunken, tattered grandeur*)
I have said I can sum it up in one single catch-all word that embraces the sentiments of everyone of these ragtails who—

COTTONMOUTH
Now shet yer grafty-phone off 'n give us the *one word*.

PERFESSER
(*Ruffled*)
Protest.

WALT
(*Weaving slightly*)
That's a good word. Yessir, I 'prove o' that word. I've done a little o' that m'self—*protest*.

SAWDUST

I protest agin' jealous husbands.

ONE-NOTE

'N railroadin' judges.

LOSER

Don't fergit race-track stewards.

BEEF

Agin' prisons, pokies, clinks, sneezers and hoosegows.

WRITER

And wardens who got more larceny in their finkin' souls than any o' the cons.

BIGAMY BOB

'N agin' women. Ever seen the figger o' justice holdin' up them scales?

SAWDUST

It's wearin' skirts 'n tippin' them scales agin' us everytime.

PERFESSER

Against law—government—morality—everything. The whole overgrown spider-web they call civilization.

COTTONMOUTH

I'm agin' everything 'ceptin' this jug, boys. Pass 'em aroun' agin'. We'll drink t'Perfesser's name fer it—er—how d'yuh say it agin'?

WALT

Protest! Good ol' protest! Here's t'protest.
WALT *has now risen, waving his jug.*

THE OTHERS

Protest. Protest! Pro-oh-test!

BEEF

What's that word mean—protest?
COTTONMOUTH *gets up—jugs in one hand, snake in the other.*

COTTONMOUTH

Here's to livin'—free! (WALT *and* COTTONMOUTH *clink jugs*) Am I right, Curley Cue the Second? (*Suddenly throws snake to* WALT) Here, you cuddle him fer a while.

With drunken, unself-conscious grace, WALT *handles the snake expertly.*

WALT

(*Doing an imitation of* COTTONMOUTH)

Been 'roun snakes all m'life. Allus have a varmint er two roun' me. Yessir, snakes is my friends—'specially if I got a firm grip on 'em.

The squatters are amused. WALT *tosses the baby snake back to* SLOW-BOY.

COTTONMOUTH

Yuh fit in like yuh was born to it. Like yuh was my kid's older brother. Only you're not—

WALT

'S funny thing. I wouldn't o' believed it. But I think this is the best ol' night of juggin' 'n jawin' I ever seed.

In wild exuberance he pours the remains of the jug over his head and dashes out into the night.

COTTONMOUTH

Boys! He's jinin' up with us! (COTTONMOUTH *follows* WALT *out onto the porch. Both are holding their jugs. The wind makes the catwalks tremble. They have to shout to be heard*) Tell yuh what I'll do with yuh, partner. I'll challenge yuh. Each man t' his own jug—'n the first one t'hit the mud has t'go out 'n wrassle Elmer the hog.

WALT

Yow-hee!

With one leap, WALT *has broad-jumped off the porch into the mud and makes his way to the homemade still near the alligator pen.* COTTONMOUTH *and his men follow, all in loud, drunken, high spirits.*

From the middle of the muddy clearing, WALT *surrounded by the squatters, raises his jug and challenges* COTTONMOUTH.

This becomes another contest in the mud, suggesting the earlier one between BEEF *and* LOSER, *only this one is being fought with moonshine and will power. But beneath the almost hysterical revelry, the underlying seriousness of the challenge is felt by all.*

COTTONMOUTH

Ya takin' on a man-sized job, boy.

Both stoop to fill their jugs at the still. From behind, THUMBS *lurches forward drunkenly with a knife, attempting to stab* WALT. COTTONMOUTH *swings his hand around violently, catching* THUMBS *in the throat.*

COTTONMOUTH

I warned ya. He belongs to me. This is a-tween two loners. (THUMBS *topples backward over the low barrier into the alligator pen. As the reptiles stir and move toward him, he screams*) All right, boys, git him out o' there afore he poisons the 'gators. (SAWDUST *and* BEEF *pull* THUMBS *out. He has suffered a wound on his hand, which everyone ignores, including* THUMBS) Next time ya act up I'll leave ya in there.

The squatters group around COTTONMOUTH *and* WALT, *egging them on as both tip their jugs to their mouths.*

THUMBS

I've got five says you'll drink 'im down.

COTTONMOUTH

That fella's bettin' on the right boy.

LOSER

Five more says you quit at the quarter pole, Bird-Boy.

WALT

You're on.

WRITER

Get ready to eat mud for a chaser.

WALT

We'll see who eats mud.

COTTONMOUTH

(*To* WALT)

My money says when I get finished with you, you won't be
able to eat nuthin'.

WALT

It's a bet.

COTTONMOUTH

Let's stop talkin' 'n start drinkin'.

WALT

Here goes, Cottonmouth. You're gonna wind up in the mud
with the rest of the snakes.

COTTONMOUTH

Three things I never turned down in my life—women, boar
meat and a dare. Man to man, whether it's jugs, guns or jes'
plain guts. 'N if ya git through this night alive le's see what
the mornin' has in store fer us. (*He lets go with a rebel yell*)
Jugs up!

> *He raises his and starts to drink lustily.* WALT *raises
> his and they drink without taking their eyes off each
> other, circling each other like fighters in a ring.*

DISSOLVE

COTTONMOUTH KEY—EARLY NEXT MORNING

WALT *is lying on a catwalk, his head hung down over the edge and resting in the mud. Slowly he rolls off the catwalk onto the ground and lies still. For a moment it seems he might be dead. But it is only drunken slumber. Like a dazed fighter, he struggles to one knee, shakes his head to get his bearings and then starts to stagger along the catwalk in the direction of* COTTONMOUTH'S *shack.*

THUMBS, ONE-NOTE *and other squatters are standing on the catwalk mending their nets. They watch him, malevolently.* WALT *staggers past them. The squatters are motionless and mute.*

At the end of the catwalk behind COTTONMOUTH'S *shack,* COTTONMOUTH *is waiting with a gun in hand, watching* WALT'S *painful approach.*

COTTONMOUTH
(*Catching him unawares*)
Mornin'. Lookin' fer a gun?
He hands the gun to WALT.

WALT
(*Taking it, his head slowly clearing*)
You're quite a fellow, Cottonmouth.

COTTONMOUTH
Are you a gambler?

WALT
Who else would take a job like this?

COTTONMOUTH
Ya take a dare pretty good. Now I'm gonna try ya on a dandy. (*Curious to see how* COTTONMOUTH *will deal with* WALT, *the squatters gather behind their leader on the porch*) If ya c'n git me into Miamuh—alive, I'll take what they got ready for me.

Only I ain't doin' nuthin' all the way 'ceptin' my fair share o' the polin' 'n I'll kill ya first chance I git—(*Pauses to study* WALT'S *reaction*) Now that's a fair offer, ain't it?

> WALT

You could have killed me right here. I figure I'm betting with your chips. What have I got to lose?

> COTTONMOUTH *smiles in appreciation of* WALT'S *adjustment to the Everglades code.*

> COTTONMOUTH

Bet! My life agin' yourn. That's the kind o' stakes I like. Le's go.

> COTTONMOUTH *and* WALT, *both with shotguns, descend the ladder of the boat-landing into* COTTONMOUTH'S *long red skiff. The squatters come forward to the edge of the porch and watch* COTTONMOUTH *with questioning eyes.*

> COTTONMOUTH

Boys, don' jes' stand aroun' waitin' fer me. Take a little run up to Duck Rock. Them birds oughta be nestin' pretty good now.

> WALT

You pole from the bow. I'll take the stern.

> COTTONMOUTH

You're the skipper, Mr. Walt. Only this time you ain't got Joe Bottles to show you the way.

> BEEF
> (*From the porch above*)

What does he keep foolin' with this apple-cheek Yankee for?

> PERFESSER
> (*Smiling slyly*)

Super-floous questions. If he's going to carry out the mission I'm sure he has in mind, why should he want us for witnesses?

WRITER

Anyone of us would turn 'im in for murder if the reward was big enough.

SAWDUST

Not me. I'm loyal.

LOSER

Loyal to your next bottle of rotgut.

PERFESSER

I wouldn't trust a single one of you seein' as I don't even trust myself.

The red skiff threads its way through the curved mangrove legs barring the approach to Cottonmouth Key.

LOSER
(Calling after him)

So long, Bird-Boy.

WRITER

We're gonna miss you.

SAWDUST

All right, boys, the boat's now leaving for Duck Rock.

On the shore, as WALT *and* COTTONMOUTH *pass,* SLOW-BOY, *assisted by* BIGAMY BOB, *is dropping the last shovelful of dirt on a small grave, crudely marked:*

PAWS PET SNAK
REST EN PECE

COTTONMOUTH

Bigamy, look after the boy. Son, if you see the Devil in the woodshed again', tell 'im yer paw inquires after his health.

SLOW-BOY
(Waving)

See ya, Paw.

COTTONMOUTH *and* WALT *pole their boat out of the man-*

grove channel into the open water of Lostman's River.
They move in the general direction of Miami.

DISSOLVE

WALT AND COTTONMOUTH—EVERGLADES
They are moving through the changing scenery of the
Glades, from the salt-water mangrove country into the
shoulder-high saw grass that marks the inner Glades.
WALT *is obviously under pressure.* COTTONMOUTH *appears*
impassive but is secretly enjoying his game of snake and
bird.

EVERGLADES—NIGHTFALL
The water is several feet deep but hidden by the relent-
less grass. There is land—hammocks—rising out of the
grass, in the far distance. WALT *has begun to show the*
effects of the journey.

WALT

It's like a mirage. I swear that hammock keeps moving away
from us.

COTTONMOUTH
(*Complacently*)

Too late to make high ground tonight. We'll have to sleep in
the boat.

WALT

Doesn't matter to me. I'm not planning to sleep.

COTTONMOUTH

That's right, yuh cain't sleep, kin yuh? It's gonna be a long
night . . . think you'll be able to stay awake?

WALT

Hope so.

COTTONMOUTH

If ya don't . . . ya'll sleep a long time. (*He settles down in the bottom of the boat, closes his eyes and sighs with exaggerated contentment*) This shut-eye is gonna feel real nice.

DISSOLVE

SAME SCENE—LATER THAT NIGHT

COTTONMOUTH *seems to be sleeping soundly. Sitting in the stern, with his shotgun for support,* WALT *nods and succumbs to sleep for a moment. He catches himself just in time, for when he looks up,* COTTONMOUTH *has opened a watchful eye. Then* COTTONMOUTH *closes his eyes again.* WALT *dabs some water on his face to stay awake.*

SAME SCENE—FIRST LIGHT OF DAWN

WALT *is hunched over on his rifle but awake, on edge after a sleepless night.* COTTONMOUTH *shifts weight.* WALT *is ready for anything he might do.* COTTONMOUTH *merely stretches and smiles disarmingly.*

COTTONMOUTH

Mornin'.

WALT

(*Begrudgingly*)

Good morning.

COTTONMOUTH

Two or three times there I was playin' possum. Figgered I'd catch ya asleep. But I didn't.

WALT

(*Rising and picking up the pole, in no mood for conversation*)

Let's get going.

COTTONMOUTH

(*With a barely perceptible grin of confidence*)

I'm ready.

117

Sunlight bathes the trackless grass in golden light.
WALT *begins to pole determinedly,* COTTONMOUTH *lacka-daisically. They move slowly on.*

DISSOLVE

EVERGLADES WATERWAYS—LATER THAT MORNING

> WALT *shows the strain of helplessness, heat, the confusion of groping his way through the marsh, and the pressure of* COTTONMOUTH's *watchful silence. Ahead are a number of forking waterways, each leading in a different direction.*

WALT
(*Half to himself*)
Now, let's see—which one of these'll take us toward—

COTTONMOUTH
Don't ask me. Ye're the skipper. Ye're the one wants t'git t'Miamuh.

WALT
(*Scanning the water and testing the bottom*)
Let's see . . . there's a hard bottom here and a tide—that means it should be the main channel—and they always run northeast—so—so I think—Miami must be this way.
He indicates the direction.

COTTONMOUTH
Are you sure o' that?

WALT
At least that's what Billy told me.
> *They start poling on, but* COTTONMOUTH *pauses a moment to think. Some unspoken attraction to this young man has been weakening his will.* WALT's *ability to adapt himself to the cruel demands of the Glades moves him to reconsider.*

COTTONMOUTH

Walt, I made up my mind. I'm not gonna kill ya. Now you take this skiff 'n head on inta Miamuh. I got my own ways o' gettin' back. Game's over!

WALT

Game's on. You made the rules. Too late to change 'em.

COTTONMOUTH

I'm givin' ya a chance, boy—but ya'll hafta gimme yer solemn word ya'll go away 'n stay away. Don'tya wanna live?

WALT

(*His nervousness somewhat belying his words*)
Stow the chatter and get movin'.

COTTONMOUTH

(*Realizing the "game" is over*)
Mr. Murdock, ye're gettin' mighty tough in yer old age, ain't-cha?

They exchange looks, having come to realize that they are locked together to the end. WALT *starts them forward with a new desperate urgency.*

DISSOLVE

A SAW-GRASS WILDERNESS

COTTONMOUTH's *skiff is a tiny object in an uncharted sea of grass.*

DISSOLVE

BIG CYPRESS SWAMP—LATE AFTERNOON

This is an eerie wonderland, a labyrinth of dark, snake-infested waterways clogged with water-hyacinth, some in blossom, and shaded by big cypress trees thickly hung with Spanish moss. The jutting, irregular "knees" of the cypress roots rise out of the water like hobgoblins. Fallen logs from impenetrable barriers, natural bridges and overhanging gardens husbanding wild orchids, scarlet Virginia creeper and other vivid tropical plants. Egrets on their stilted legs stalk the teeming waters of the swamp in search of minnows. The startling wood ibis watch from the topmost branches of the thousand-year-old cypress. The incessant drilling of shrill, brilliantly colored woodpeckers reveals their disregard for antiquity. A great blue heron sweeps past. But the unique beauty of a big cypress swamp is lost on WALT, *for all his naturalist sensibilities. The stubborn dam of overgrown hyacinth blocks the onward passage of the skiff. Fighting exhaustion and despair, he attempts to push the matted hyacinth aside with his pole, but it will not give.* COTTONMOUTH *simply sits there with poker-faced confidence like a buzzard waiting for his victim to drop.*

WALT
(*Wearily pulling his pole back into the skiff again*)
Well, I guess it's get out and walk again.

COTTONMOUTH
In the Glades, sometimes the longest way around is the shortest way through.

WALT
What are you trying to say?

COTTONMOUTH
You figger it out.

WALT
(*Jumping into the water and pushing the skiff from behind. The water is up to his waist*)
Listen, Cottonmouth, I know what you're doing—trying to get me lost. I know the best way back is through this—(*Pushing with what remains of his strength*) I've got to get through this.

COTTONMOUTH

(*Turning to look at him from his seat in the prow*)
Walt, if ya could use the brains God give ya you'd steer clear o' this stretch.

WALT

(*Fighting hysteria*)
I say we cut through here.

COTTONMOUTH

Can't make it.

WALT

Get out and help me push and we'll make it.

COTTONMOUTH

Oh, no—all I said is I'd do my fair share o' the polin'. I ain't wettin' my feet.

WALT

Then you pole and I'll push. (*Grabbing his gun and waving it at* COTTONMOUTH, *screaming at him*) Now get leanin' on that mud-pusher. Go on—pole!

COTTONMOUTH

Ya wet-behind-the-ears Yankee schoolboy, ya ain't got me inta Miamuh yet.
He gets up and takes the pole, using it perfunctorily.

WALT

(*His voice breaking a little with desperation*)
Pole!—I said pole!

COTTONMOUTH *starts to pole and* WALT *presses his chest against the stern, with feverish energy. The skiff inches forward.* WALT *scans the brackish water, and moves cautiously but steadily on.*

WALT *sees a number of sinuous water moccasins (the deadly cottonmouth) swimming away from him in the water. Another moccasin, with half a dozen poisonous offspring, writhes on an overhanging branch. In his exhaustion* WALT *begins to tremble with the effort of forcing the boat through this water-logged jungle. His eyes look crazed. He stares at* COTTONMOUTH *and he sees a distorted giant figure. The cypress limbs and the apparitional Spanish moss revolve around him in a nightmare kaleidoscope. Over* COTTONMOUTH's *right shoulder he thinks he sees a six-foot snake on a tree limb, ready to strike. He fires crazily at the "snake"—which turns out to be only the twisted vine of a strangler fig. The shot narrowly misses* COTTONMOUTH. *Instinctively, with all his animal strength, he swings his gnarled buttonwood pole at* WALT, *smashing him into the water. In a rage he swings a second time, cracking the pole against* WALT's *left shoulder. He is about to club* WALT *again when he hears his scream—*

WALT

Snake—I thought it was a snake!

Only now does COTTONMOUTH *see the driftwood "snake" floating near* WALT.

Realizing his mistake, COTTONMOUTH *jumps out of the boat into the water and carries the injured* WALT *toward a cypress tree against which a fallen trunk is leaning.*

COTTONMOUTH

(*After putting* WALT *down and bathing his wound*)

Walt, I kept hopin' I wouldn't hafta hurt ya. When I heard that shot I figgered ya was aimin' t'kill me. I ain't never done nothin' I was sorry fer, 'ceptin' this. I'm bone sorry fer this.

WALT

(*With pain*)

I guess you win. The Glades are all yours.

COTTONMOUTH

I coulda told ya that the first day ya come in.

Overhead a flock of white egrets are flying. The sound of their wings attracts WALT. *He looks up through the cypress branches into the sky.*

WALT

Can't you see they're beautiful? Why can't people just enjoy them 'nstead of killing them . . . enjoy them—be thankful for them . . .

COTTONMOUTH

Guess I'll never get it through my head why ya keep takin' such chances fuh birds.

WALT

(*His eyes soaring with them*)
See how the sun catches their wings?

COTTONMOUTH

(*Compassion is wrung from him as* WALT *grimaces with pain*)
Guess I'll hafta pole ya into Miamuh.

WALT

I'll still have to turn you in. You know that.

COTTONMOUTH

(*Affected by* WALT's *outrageous spirit*)
Ya feel gut-deep 'bout livin', don'tcha—like me. I'll take ya in.

COTTONMOUTH *rises from the log to reach for the bowline of the skiff that has fallen into the water. As he dips his hand into the brackish water a cottonmouth snake strikes from below the surface.* COTTONMOUTH *pulls his hand out with the snake still fastened to the artery of his wrist with its fangs. He bellows a terrible cry of pain.*

COTTONMOUTH
(*With a wild sense of irony*)
Bite deep, Brother! Bite deep! (*He flings the snake from him; it swims away. Moaning deeply, tightly holding his wrist,* COTTONMOUTH *wades over to the cypress log and slumps down. His head has broken out in sweat but he struggles to hold it high.* WALT *rises, with effort, and wades over to him*) Walt, I never figgered natural causes'd do me in first.

WALT
There's nothing in here strong enough to kill you.

COTTONMOUTH
(*Trembling with the tremendous effort to maintain his dignity*)
The Glades are stronger 'n anything.

WALT
(*Rushing toward him*)
A knife—maybe I can cut out the . . .

COTTONMOUTH
(*Thrusting* WALT *away from him*)
Too late! It's already in my blood. Ya better git goin', boy. When ya come to the last big cypress—ya was right, ya was right—ya'll hit a channel that'll ride ya in.

WALT
I can't leave you here alone.

COTTONMOUTH
I got plenty o' company. Now git goin'!

WALT
Don't tell me—I can't—I've got to stay with you.

COTTONMOUTH
(*Bellowing*)
When I say git goin'! (*His voice rises to an overpowering roar*) I mean *GIT GOIN'!*

The shout is so loud that it frightens the egrets, who begin to fill the sky. WALT *looks at* COTTONMOUTH *and sees in his strong, dimming eyes that this is a man who demands and deserves the right to die on his own terms.* WALT *turns slowly away from* COTTONMOUTH *and wades out toward the skiff.*

Sinking down closer to the water, COTTONMOUTH *inadvertently looks up at the birds, his eyes seeming to take in the beauty of them for the first time.*

COTTONMOUTH
(Muttering)

Mebbe ye're right. Mebbe I never took a real good look at 'em before—(*He looks up again and sees some black buzzards flying through the flock of white egrets. He gathers his strength for one last act of defiance, and, still holding the fatal wound, he rises to shout a final challenge into the sky*) Come 'n git me—swamp-born 'n swamp-fattened, tough 'n tasty Glades meat!

He falls back, dead. The waning sunlight, filtering through the trees, highlights his fiery beard, his monumental head.

COTTONMOUTH *is sinking back into the Glades out of which he came. Beyond,* WALT *is painfully trying to pole* COTTONMOUTH'S *skiff on through the cypress swamp into the clearing. His left arm hangs limp at his side. When he hears* COTTONMOUTH'S *final cry, he doesn't look back, but his face begins to struggle against the repressed tears. He poles on, out of the shadows, into the late afternoon sunlight that can transform a dark and deadly cypress swamp into a garden spot of hyacinth blossoms, water the color of liquid gold, and birds immaculately white, heavenly blue and indescribably carmine, filling the sunset sky.*

As WALT *poles on, still hoping to reach Miami, a thousand birds, then five thousand, ten thousand—as number-*

less, as necessary, as eternal as the stars—fill the skies over the Everglades. And superimposed over the dissolving images of birds in flight, these words appear:

IN MEMORY OF THE AUDUBON WARDENS WHO RISKED AND EVEN GAVE THEIR LIVES TO KEEP THE PLUME BIRDS OF AMERICA HIGH-FLYING AND FREE

FADE OUT

THE END